TOWER

BAE MYUNG-HOON

Translated by Sung Ryu

Honford
Star

This translation first published by Honford Star 2020
honfordstar.com
© Bae Myung-hoon 2009
Translation copyright © Sung Ryu 2020
All rights reserved
The moral right of the translator and editors has been asserted.

ISBN (paperback): 978-1-9162771-2-0
ISBN (ebook): 978-1-9162771-3-7
A catalogue record for this book is available from the British Library.

Printed and bound in Paju, South Korea
Cover illustration by Jisu Choi
Typeset by Honford Star

This book is published with the support of the
Literature Translation Institute of Korea (LTI Korea).

CONTENTS

Three Wise Recruits

The Version Including the Dog

Some liquors serve as currency. In life, there are times when one must give something to someone with no guarantee of getting anything in return. This is different from giving bribes, kickbacks, payoffs, or sweeteners, in which cases what to give is fairly straightforward and what to get in exchange is crystal clear. But in payment-for-service relationships that involve far more delicate and sensitive mechanisms, like offering a "token of gratitude" or a "little something," what that subtle gift might be and what is expected in return are not specified explicitly. This is intentional, leaving a way out should things go awry. That is how power usually works, except in emergencies.

Professor Jung of Beanstalk Tacit Power Research, who learned early in his career how difficult it is to choose a gift that caters perfectly to the recipient's tastes in such delicate exchanges, investigated how people dealt with the problem.

"That fucking auditor the client sent us, I have no idea how to grease his palm," Professor Jung told his colleague at the research center. "Who does he think he is, a saint? What did Vertical Transportation Research buy him with? Should I give him tea or something? Or ginseng? Hell, should I just load him up with cash?"

Of course, the professor knew he shouldn't do that. Straight cash was never an option, however desperate one might be for a medium of exchange as universal as money. In all eras and cultures, using cash in such delicate relationships has been taken as cheating. If one were to be caught, cash would be the most incriminating evidence there is. So, how were people dealing with this problem? Professor Jung pondered over this question, searching far and wide for new currencies that worked admirably in such situations. He discovered quite a few—one of which was liquor.

For liquor to serve as currency, its value as a gift must stay above a certain baseline regardless of whom one gives it to and what their tastes are. It should be a universal medium of exchange that pleases even those who already own the same product, should not run the risk of offending recipients for religious or ethical reasons, and should hold some value even for non-drinkers. This is how liquor functions when it qualifies as currency.

Of course, not all liquor qualifies. Based on two decades of primary data collected on his political connections, Professor Jung ruminated on what types of liquor ultimately acquire the status of currency: "First, it has to be the kind of liquor that everybody raves about, and it doesn't matter if they don't know why. How many people can tell apart a twenty-year-old whisky from a thirty-year-old one just by taste? Older liquor is more expensive, so people buy it thinking it's better."

"Is it really better?" asked Dr. Lee.

"Sure," replied Professor Jung. "You don't buy that kind of liquor to drink at home by yourself—you only buy it when you need to show off. People think, 'How expensive can a bottle be?' But when you actually have to pay, it's a lot of money. Which is why most people never have an expensive bottle of liquor lying around the house unless it was a gift. And even if it had been a gift, you wouldn't drink it. You'd re-gift it. There's always occasion to visit someone's house, and you can't go empty-handed even if you were invited on short notice, can you?"

"So, it circulates. That means a bottle you give can come back full circle?"

"Correct," said Professor Jung.

Dr. Lee was already in his third year at Beanstalk Tacit Power Research. Listening to Professor Jung talk, he couldn't decide if the man was a genius or a crook. But when Professor Jung announced one day that he would spend the equipment budget on three cases of hard liquor, Dr. Lee thought he finally had some measure of what this man was: a nutcase. But this conviction faltered when Dr. Lee heard how the liquor would be used. After pointing out that the liquor wasn't any old liquor but the strongest gifting currency in Beanstalk of late, Professor Jung argued that if he put electronic tags on every bottle, entered them into the upper echelons of Beanstalkian society, and closely tracked their circulation, he would eventually get a distribution map of tacit power within the building. This was indeed a convincing hypothesis. So much so that the client who commissioned this research wound up approving the absurdity of purchasing three cases of thirty-five-year-old liquor with the research funds.

When he got his hands on the liquor, Professor Jung popped open a bottle for a "quality check," handed around a glass to each researcher in broad daylight, and, his face flushed brick-red, rambled on about which parts of the research required the most careful execution.

"The liquor will circulate by itself sooner or later, but we could get completely different results depending on what channels we use to introduce the bottles into the system. So, my guess is that the initial distribution phase will be the most important. Am I right?"

Everyone nodded. It was decided that Professor Jung would personally execute the distribution phase.

"And bear in mind that the researcher's actions should not influence the subjects," added Professor Jung. "It's common sense really, but we should preserve the power structure of Beanstalk exactly as is while we conduct the research. Down to the smallest detail. Got it?"

Everyone nodded again. It was decided that Professor Jung would take all the bottles home and, when the holidays came around, casually send them out to people he needed to express his gratitude to, like he always did. He also ordered customized stickers for electronic tagging.

"I already know what to write on the stickers: *Military Distribution Only*. Nice, huh? Just stick that on the bottle and its value jumps by fifty percent."

And so the research kicked off. It would be carried out over a year and a half. The first batch of liquor was distributed fifteen days before the holidays, after which the research team took daily 3D scans of the entire building to track each bottle. But soon Professor Jung claimed it was ludicrous to track the power structure of a 674-story building with a population of 500,000 using only three cases of liquor, and he ordered five more. Professor Jung added that while Beanstalk may look small, it was a globally recognized sovereign state whose power structure was not so rudimentary.

When the client's audit team asked why Professor Jung had to distribute the liquor in such small batches every day over several months instead of doing one mass distribution, he shot back angrily, "I told you—this is currency. What happens when you issue too much money? Inflation, right? This isn't the only gifting currency out there: there's five more. If this currency inflates, it would mess up the exchange rate with the other currencies. Then we might have to start the research all over again. How does it make any sense to throw away our research funds like that?"

Dr. Lee watched this exchange in silence. He was at a loss for words.

Professor Jung was out of the office every day distributing the newly procured liquor. He clocked in around lunchtime and clocked out at dinnertime, but he always made a point of submitting overtime requests. The other researchers were not happy about that, but no one could deny Professor Jung's talent for doling out "little somethings" to a vast number of people surrounding the locus of power, and God knows how he managed to get in with them in the first place. As Professor Jung had pointed out, failing to properly introduce the liquor would skew the results, so his colleagues had no choice but to trust him with the job. No one else could do it.

The research was on a tight schedule that required the final report to be written up before the Beanstalk mayoral elections in March. The results therefore had to be finalized by late January to allow time for drafting the report. There were five categories to track other than liquor, and by observing the flow of the six categories, the client wanted to understand how power in the current mayor's regime was structured and exploit those findings in the last stretch of the election campaign—the client being the opposition's campaign. It seemed the opposition campaign already had an ace up its sleeve but had commissioned the research to secure definitive evidence. That put more pressure on Dr. Lee. The client's impress-me attitude made it hard for him to take any part of his work lightly.

The researchers were also tasked with creating an elaborate 3D illustration of Beanstalk's power distribution by early January. Perhaps this was more important than writing the report itself, as they lived in a world where citable images were more important than the research findings. So, in reality, the research had to be wrapped up by the end of December, and even if they did not have the final results by then, they needed conclusions that were relatively accurate.

When December rolled around, everyone except Professor Jung began working around the clock, punching in early and punching out late. Professor Jung, meanwhile, hired three young PhDs from outside Beanstalk, all barely over the age of thirty, leaving him free to continue what he had been doing—that is to say, not much.

Dr. Lee asked the three new recruits, "Did Professor Jung at least say he'd give you part-time wages?"

"Excuse me? Did you just say part-time? Are we not on payroll?" asked Dr. Song, one of the new researchers.

Heaving a sigh, Dr. Lee skimmed over their personnel files. "I see Dr. Song Yunjoo majored in power field analytics, Dr. Nam Sungho did skyscraper ecology, and Dr. Hwang Yunjin—wait, you did your PhD on World War I?"

"Yes."

"That's unusual. I don't mean it's unusual for a female researcher to major in war, I'm just wondering why someone with that specialization would come here."

"Beats me. I'm not sure myself why he called me in," admitted Dr. Hwang.

Things were busy but with the deadlines being manageable, Dr. Lee did not plan on assigning especially difficult tasks to the three new recruits, nor did he feel the need to hire more backup staff as he didn't foresee any emergencies arising. But no sooner had December arrived than Dr. Lee ran into an unexpected problem.

"A57 on Level 487, whose house is this?" he asked.

Dr. Lee had found a unit where the liquor wasn't moving with the natural flow of the power structure. The inhabitant of unit A57 on Level 487 appeared to have blocked the flow. Given that five bottles had flowed into the unit in the past ten days, whoever lived there was evidently an important person. But as all five bottles went in and never came back out, the inhabitant had to be either someone at the pinnacle of power or a binge drinker.

Although the liquor had acquired the status of currency, Dr. Lee could not say for certain it would keep circulating without ever being consumed at some point. Yet so many bottles gathering so quickly at one place and not moving a single unit further was definitely abnormal. The inhabitant could be out of town, or there could be numerous other explanations. In any case, first and foremost Dr. Lee had to check on the situation and clear the blockage.

To trace the inhabitant's identity, Dr. Lee consulted the resident directory that Professor Jung had obtained a while back by bribing a senior employee of the Security Guard-house. All he found listed in the directory was "Film Actor P." Deciding that sorting things out in person would be faster, Dr. Lee hopped into an elevator and headed up to Level 487. Levels 27 and 487 were so far apart that he had to change elevators six times.

When Dr. Lee arrived at unit A57 on Level 487, it became obvious why the liquor had hit a dead end. Film Actor P was not human. He was canine.

Dr. Lee was appalled. A dog could not possibly drink thirty-five-year-old liquor. Why would anyone send liquor to a dog? And five bottles at that.

Going straight back to the research center, Dr. Lee looked

for Professor Jung. As he had expected, his boss had left work early so he phoned Professor Jung and gave him the full story, then asked whether or not the dog should be included in the power network analysis. Professor Jung chided him with a mildly indignant air.

"Oh come on, drunk people do stupid things, but to call them a dog? An educated man like yourself should know better."

Dr. Lee explained that no, that was not what he had meant, people were sending liquor to a real dog, the kind that walked on four legs.

The news did not seem to surprise Professor Jung very much. On the contrary, he barked, "Of course we should exclude the dog. We're not zoologists, are we? This is a power field we're talking about."

However, Dr. Lee knew that this being a power field was precisely the problem. If the research was simply about determining who had power, taking one dog out of the picture was fine. But a power field is a different story. It is like a gravitational field, where a celestial object warps the space around it due to its mass. When massless particles of light pass through the warped space, they cannot travel in a straight line and are instead refracted by it. Power fields work the same way. When power warps the very space around it, creating a power field, even people who believe they are impervious to power begin to show signs of caving in to it and start acting as if they are consciously trying to please it. Whether people intend to cave in to power or not, their actions appear more or less the same to an outside observer. According to this power field theory, a dog could very well end up in the locus of power.

Dr. Lee considered what results he would get if he excluded Film Actor P. Using the data he had so far, he simulated Beanstalk's power structure after five holiday seasons into the future. The structure evolved into completely different shapes depending on whether or not the dog was included. Without the dog, several loci of power besides the existing one appeared sporadically between the middle floors and the rich neighborhood on the top floor, then disappeared. With the dog, however, the locus of power became a neat sphere with a nucleus centered on the City Hall complex on the middle floors. That model was true to life.

The following afternoon, Dr. Lee went to see Professor Jung and voiced his concerns. But the professor wouldn't budge.

"Be that as it may, we can't write that in the report," Professor Jung said. "What would we tell the client, 'Hey, Beanstalk's power network has a dog in it, and there's no way we can finish the research if we exclude the dog'?"

"Why not?" asked Dr. Lee. "I don't see the harm in telling them. We wouldn't tell the newspapers."

"We wouldn't, but how do you know *they* wouldn't? 'The mayor's key power source is a dog!' The papers would have a field day. And let's say the mayor gets re-elected, are we going to close the research center?"

"But this isn't something we can categorically exclude. We don't know why, but we can't deny the power field bends in that direction. Without the dog, there'd be many things we can't explain."

"Then just say it's a person. Do we really need to specify it's a dog?"

"It wouldn't make sense for the liquor bottles to keep going into a person's house but not out, unless that person was pretty high up. But not disclosing who it is would look suspicious. If you were the opposition's campaign team, would you let something like that slide? You'd start sniffing around."

"I don't care. Just exclude it."

"I'm afraid I can't," Dr. Lee declared. "If you're going ahead with this, I'm out."

In the end, Professor Jung kicked Dr. Lee off his team, which presented a serious setback to the research timeline. The three new recruits had to now help out in earnest.

"It's nothing too difficult," said Dr. Lee airily. "Just simple tabulation. Well, you'll have to crunch a year's worth of data. Call if there's anything weird."

However, the work proved anything but simple. Although Dr. Lee's work was now split between Dr. Song, Dr. Hwang, and Dr. Nam, they had no clue what they were doing.

Beanstalk was an environment they had never seen before; it seemed spatially impossible. The number 674 for starters. Instead of 674 spaces lying neatly on top of each other in clearly defined floors, oddly-shaped spaces like Tetris blocks were piled to a height commensurate with 674 floors, so you could not say for sure how many floors the building had. The total number of floors changed depending on where you started counting.

The specialist was none the wiser. Dr. Nam said, "My expertise doesn't help much here. You just don't see buildings like this in skyscraper ecology. Normal skyscrapers are occupied only during working hours. The buildings have a primary purpose and most of their occupants work there for that purpose. The rest are cleaning and maintenance, et cetera. You should be able to make that sort of distinction, but folks here never leave the building—they live in it. Anyway, Dr. Song you're the power field analysis expert. Shouldn't this stuff be right up your alley?"

"It should be, but I've never done anything like this either." replied Dr. Song. "I have to draw a power field in 3D. The city center should also be 3D, but I honestly can't picture a power field bending itself around a locus of power in 3D. In 2D, you can think of a locus of power as putting a heavy object on a flat plane. Then that point would sag down, right? A downhill would form, pulling everything to the bottom. Now *that* I can picture intuitively, but to translate it to 3D is beyond me."

Dr. Hwang chimed in, "So imagine what it's like for me. I'm a military history major, and I've no idea why I'm here. At the end of the year too."

"You did say your father's a friend of Professor Jung," Dr. Song said.

"Yes, but still."

Whether it was doable or not, they had to pull it off. And do it well.

The days rolled on. When the holidays arrived, the building exterior was covered with dazzling decorations. Beanstalk

Tower wasn't a pencil-thin skyscraper, but a thick one in both length and width. Adverts that hung on its outer walls were visible to everyone—everyone in the neighboring capital, that is, not to Beanstalk residents. The adverts were so massive and placed so high up that no one could avoid looking at them. They reduced the amount of sunlight entering Beanstalk and lowered the temperature of many levels inside, but that was a sacrifice worth making for the enormous ad revenues. Level 27, where Beanstalk Tacit Power Research was situated, was one of the affected levels.

Dr. Song was blowing warm air on her hands as she stared dully into the monitor, when she suddenly looked around at her two colleagues. "Shouldn't we go visit?"

Dr. Nam replied, "Why should we? We're not exactly close to him."

"Professor Jung said his wife insisted we come, remember?"

"She couldn't have. She doesn't know us. It was just a polite thing to say."

"She came for a visit once. When you weren't here. Dr. Hwang and I met her. She seemed glad to meet people her own age. I bet that's why she's asked us to come over. So let's go?"

Dr. Nam replied, "If we had time on our hands, sure, but we're swamped."

"Oh, come on," Dr. Song tried again.

But like Dr. Nam said, their work was nowhere near finished. Although they had intended to wrap up the project by now, the research was not going as planned. As the year came to a close, "gestures of goodwill" were exchanged much more than usual, giving the researchers exponentially more data to track.

Dr. Song looked up anxiously at the clock. "Wouldn't it look bad if we don't go and everyone else does?" she asked.

"Please, you know people don't visit new mothers for three weeks after they give birth," said Dr. Nam.

"Apparently you do here," said Dr. Song. "I heard you don't actually see the mother or the baby, you just need to leave a gift and make an appearance. Everyone else said they're going."

"Because they have less work than we do," said Dr. Nam. "You want to come in tomorrow too?"

Dr. Song replied, "You're right. There's no way I'm coming in on Christmas, I'm not even getting paid. Forget it."

Professor Jung had not made the slightest mention of salary, but the three researchers still had to do a proper job. However unfair, they had to do it to stay on his good side. Get on his wrong side, and they had no hope of surviving in academia. They could not show their displeasure or slack off, and if anyone asked about the research, all they could say was it made for a great learning experience. Professor Jung may not have enough clout to help them achieve success, but he had enough clout to stand in their way of it. If they harbored any ambition of landing, say, a faculty job in Beanstalk University's political science department, they had to work without complaining.

"Wish they'd turn on the heaters at least." Dr. Song wrapped her shoulders with a purple blanket someone had taken from a plane and gazed blankly at her monitor. This was usually

Professor Jung's job. Notorious as he was for shirking his work, the professor had nevertheless gotten a little done each day, but today he had gone straight to the hospital first thing. Declaring that his wife, or more precisely his second wife who was seventeen years his junior, had gone into labor, he took three whole days off when everybody else was so busy. As if that wasn't enough, he invited all his colleagues to the hospital to see the baby. It was a strange custom. He could of course take leave, but Dr. Song didn't understand why Professor Jung had to invite other people.

"Still, shouldn't we go?" asked Dr. Song again.

With a hint of impatience, Dr. Nam replied, "We've no business going there, alright? It's bad enough a man his age was cheating with a young woman, but to get her pregnant, dump his wife, and marry her? I saw him all jittery, like a first-time dad in his twenties. As if. The guy's got three kids already. Even I was embarrassed for him."

"But isn't that why that woman's making a point of inviting everyone over?" asked Dr. Song. "So people like you don't say how embarrassing they are behind their backs. I'm telling you—they're writing a hit list. I say now's the time for us pop in and present ourselves."

Dr. Nam said, "If you finish that model today, I'll go with you."

Dr. Song turned back around. She did not feel like rushing on Christmas Eve just to see someone's wife and their new baby. Rushing wouldn't help her suddenly solve the problems she had been struggling with anyway. Dr. Song stared at her screen, perturbed. Looking closely at Level 100, something seemed off there, but she couldn't quite put her finger on it.

Common sense told Dr. Song that Beanstalk's locus of power should rest between Levels 250 and 350, where the city's administrative center was nestled in the shape of a sphere. There were a few anomalies, but they were explainable—all but one. A highly concentrated locus of power sat on the northeastern outskirts of the region between Levels 90 and 130, but she didn't have the faintest idea why a locus would form there.

Dr. Song lapsed into deep thought. Even after going through the primary data again Dr. Song found no answers. She could only guess. Perhaps there was a gang, a local big shot, or some other explanation everybody knew about except out-of-towners like her. She couldn't expect to solve the mystery by the end of the day.

"Hey Dr. Nam. See this area here?" asked Dr. Song. "Near Level 100, right at this edge. It's super concentrated, but I can't for the life of me figure out why."

Dr. Nam examined the screen and thumbed through pages of data in search of causes, but he couldn't pinpoint a satisfactory explanation either. "I don't know, maybe the mayor's lover lives there. Shouldn't we ask a local? Professor Jung's our best bet if we want the dirt on someone."

Dr. Song asked, "Shall we call?"

Professor Jung did not pick up, to no one's surprise. After debating what to do, Dr. Song called Dr. Lee, who fortunately answered. In a voice that was neither annoyed nor overpleased by her call, Dr. Lee told her about the dog that lived on Level 487.

"I don't know what the professor's thinking," said Dr. Lee. "When you run the simulation without the dog, you keep getting the locus of power at odd points, right? When I did it, the locus would appear on higher floors, but I guess you'd get different patterns every time you input more data. At the end of the day though, Professor Jung should be the one to deal with that. Seeing as the research will be published under his name. If any problems come up later, this isn't something he can blame you folks for."

Dr. Song said, "Professor Jung's not in right now. He's been at the hospital since morning."

"Ah, that woman's having her baby? I heard she used to be a singer, or maybe an actor? A celebrity that never made it big. She's not keeping the news hush-hush then. Anyway, I can't tell you what to do. What if I did and something were to go wrong? Suppose you say you did it because I told you to, where would that put me? Get a definite answer out of Professor Jung. Or don't do any more work until he has to do it himself."

Dr. Song hung up and turned wearily back to her screen. She told the other two about what she had discussed with Dr. Lee, but most of it was lost on them because it involved too much power field analysis jargon.

"I'm not a big fan of computerizing research," said Dr. Hwang. "I don't think we understood anything you just said. Looks like you're on your own, Dr. Song."

Dr. Song certainly had no qualms about computerized research or computers that learn. If anything, she rather trusted them. Although she didn't dare mention this to the other two, Dr. Song thought that taking a power field analysis program typically used on 2D city structures and repurposing it for a 3D space like Beanstalk was an achievement by Professor Jung that deserved some credit.

"We should create two versions. One with the dog, one without," she announced.

This was a reckless decision. They already had enough on their plates, but Dr. Song was now suggesting they double their workload. Despite furious protests from Dr. Hwang and Dr. Nam, Dr. Song had made up her mind and hurriedly set to work.

Dr. Song said, "This needs to be finished today no matter what."

Even though the research used computer models, inputting data did not automatically crank out results. Computerized research was only a tool, one that required humans to constantly monitor and tweak. It made a great instrument if used well, but it was complicated to employ correctly. Dr. Song began to input the data, including the trajectory of liquor bottles that flowed into unit A57 on Level 487. As reference points, Dr. Song used five projection models created from tracking other currency-goods such as concert ticket vouchers, red ginseng gift sets, and fountain pens, and punched in each of their reference priorities and confidence levels. That was not something a computer could do for her; the process relied entirely on Dr. Song's judgment.

As she worked, Dr. Song had doubts about whether making two versions was a wise decision. But she had gone too far to turn back now. Initially she stayed on top of which variables to track, but as the number of variables grew, she missed more things. The number of errors snowballed. Dr. Song struggled with the massive ball of errors weighing down her shoulders. If she fixed one error, another popped up. But with time, she solved problems faster than the rate at which new ones occurred. Not fast enough, however. The problem was time.

After three hours, Dr. Song had produced a workable model. By now everyone else had left and they were the last three in the research center.

"Almost done!" Dr. Song said.

Dr. Nam and Dr. Hwang came over to survey her screen. Dr. Nam asked, "So can we go home now?"

"No. I have to repeat what I've done one more time."

Dr. Song's heart was heavy. She wished she had made the version without A57 first. Then she could have called it a day and gone home. But it felt good to have completed something. Besides, this version was closer to the truth: power including the dog.

The three of them huddled around the monitor and examined the true power structure of Beanstalk Tower. With a crisply defined center and periphery, it looked much cleaner than any model they had pored over so far. This was how true power should be. Somehow, power did not seem like true power when it was complicated, scattered, and fraught with competition. They were no advocates of authoritarianism, but as researchers, simple things sometimes struck them as more beautiful.

"Looks great, but how do you read this thing?" asked Dr. Hwang.

"Well. Frankly, I'm not sure myself," replied Dr. Song.

A silence fell. No one spoke for five whole minutes until Dr. Hwang said, "Brighter colors mean higher concentration, right?"

"Yes," said Dr. Song. "I'm not saying the concentration of goods or people is actually high there, I'm speaking theoretically. The idea is to work backwards, so if the goods are refracted at a point, then we assume power is concentrated there."

"Does this line show how the power space is warped?" asked Dr. Hwang.

"Yes, it's an imaginary line," answered Dr. Song. "But it should be pretty accurate as we have the data to support it."

"I'm no expert but this part right here, where it's bright, where it's sticking out a little. Isn't that near Professor Jung's place? Maybe I'm wrong, but it seems like it."

Dr. Song riffled through the building's resident directory. It did seem like it. That was also where all the researchers had convened for the first time before the liquor was distributed. Dr. Song checked Professor Jung's address, which tallied with where Dr. Hwang had indicated. A thin line extended from the locus of power to a point just above Level 190. Professor Jung's address was M225 on Level 193, precisely at that point.

"That's odd," said Dr. Hwang. Odd indeed. Dr. Song zoomed in on the point. She was aware of Professor Jung's influence in academia, but he wasn't important enough to cause such a wide angle of refraction as she saw on the screen. What was more, the refracted line was long and ran in one direction, which was not a typical pattern of power.

Dr. Song reviewed the data again. She had not forgotten to account for the fact that Professor Jung distributed the liquor. That variable was eliminated. In other words, sometime after the initial distribution, more goods must have flowed into the unit.

But the movement of goods was bizarre. In the enlarged image, Dr. Song saw that a path formed between A1 on Level 339.7 and M225 on Level 193. In theory, A1 on Standard Level 339.7 was at the heart of Beanstalk's power structure, yet strangely enough, M225 was pulling goods directly from there. The goods were leaving a highly concentrated source of top power in A1, so the weighted value of each was staggeringly high, even though there weren't large quantities of them.

Dr. Song asked "What the devil could this mean? Dr. Nam, do you know if Professor Jung's friendly with the mayor?"

"He can't be," replied Dr. Nam. "At least not to that extent anyway. The mayor's not on the list of people he sent holiday gifts to. Which means they're not acquainted."

"Exactly. But you know what this looks like? Like something has stuck its hand into a black hole and snatched out a star that had been sucked in. If this thing were a person, it'd be a robber, so to speak. Or a secret lover?"

As soon as Dr. Song finished speaking, a hush fell over them. A secret lover! It wasn't impossible.

"Are you saying Professor Jung is seeing the mayor?" asked Dr. Hwang.

Dr. Song and Dr. Nam looked at her in exasperation.

"No, that's not who I meant," said Dr. Song.

Dr. Hwang thumped the desk as if she had finally cottoned on.

"Hang on, can it be Professor Jung's new wife? She wasn't a superstar, but she was relatively famous. She used to turn up in the tabloids once in a while, but then disappeared one day, right?"

Relapsing into silence, they racked their brains. They had clearly discovered something, but they needed more time to deduce what the implications would be.

"Professor Jung will have a fit if he finds out," said Dr. Hwang.

Dr. Song was about to call Professor Jung when a thought occurred to her and she put the receiver back down. After all, Professor Jung was not the main problem. The mayor was who really mattered. He was not guaranteed re-election, but he was a politician whose approval ratings were still fairly high.

They considered how Professor Jung's wife could help them. Nothing in particular came to mind. But that was how a power field worked. It was not an express contractual relationship in which one paid for specific services; it was a delicate, curious equation in which variables like simple gestures of goodwill or one extra face-to-face interaction may someday result in an unexpected boon. To solve that equation, elaborate and precise calculation was far less important than tact and timing.

"Mrs. Jung insisted we visit, you say?" asked Dr. Hwang. They had to choose a ladder to climb. Should they tell Professor Jung about their discovery, or pretend it never happened?

It did not take them long to decide. Whichever ladder they chose, the person they would meet at the top was not Professor Jung but his wife.

"I guess we'll have to drop by the hospital?" said Dr. Song.

The other two nodded.

"Let's keep this under wraps," said Dr. Song, pointing at her monitor. "If this gets out, the mayor's going to be obliterated in this election." Then, she quickly backed up her work. She had no intention of making any threats, but she wanted to keep some evidence of how they were helping the mayor. She added, "I'll come in tomorrow to create a different model to be used in the final report. Is that alright with you? And you?"

"Absolutely," the other two replied.

The hospital was on Level 647, near the rich district. Earlier that December, construction had begun on Beanstalk's rooftop of an installation that had the shape of a giant. The residents, however, recalled not the giant from the building's namesake fairytale, "Jack and the Beanstalk," but King Kong. Yet once the figure was painted, it turned out to be Santa Claus. The three recruits had to go nearly all the way up to where that giant Santa hung to get to the hospital.

Situated on Level 27, Beanstalk Tacit Power Research sat a little above the visa-free levels. The basement floors had never been Beanstalk territory, and Levels 1 to 12 comprised a single large garden. Above the garden was the Middle Zone, or Demilitarized Zone, where foreigners were free to enter—commercial facilities such as department stores, malls, and movie theaters all the way up to Level 21. Then, Levels 22 to

25 were dedicated to the Security Guardhouse, effectively forming Beanstalk's national border with six border checkpoints and two thousand of Beanstalk Army's twenty-two hundred soldiers.

That the border consisted of four levels was a mark of how many enemies had their sights on Beanstalk. After two attempted bombings by terrorists, Beanstalk expanded its border from one floor—Level 22—to four. If hostile relations with Cosmomafia continued, Beanstalk Tacit Power Research may well be included in the border before long.

The trio packed their things and set out to the nearest shopping mall. As prices above the border were too high, they did not dare shop for a gift to take to the hospital there. So, they crossed the border and took the elevator down to the entrance of a mall on Level 19.

"Let's meet back here in half an hour," said Dr. Song. "I'm getting a gold ring. You know the Beanstalkian custom is to give babies a ring at birth instead of their first birthday, right? You two get something other than a ring. Good luck picking your gifts and see you back here in thirty."

Dr. Song disappeared into the mall before anyone else could speak.

"Not cool, calling dibs on the ring. She just doesn't want to have to worry about what to buy," said Dr. Nam, staring about him, unsure of what to buy. When he spotted a perfume shaped like a mini liquor bottle at a nearby fragrance store, he grabbed it without a second thought.

"I'll just go with this. It looks like one of our liquor bottles," Dr. Nam told Dr. Hwang.

Dr. Hwang, who had been wandering in and out of stores indecisively, decided to make another quick round just as they were due to meet Dr. Song. And sure enough, Dr. Song promptly appeared, muttering about how buying the ring was an easy choice but she had dug her own grave because gold prices had skyrocketed. When Dr. Hwang returned, she had something in her hand.

Dr. Nam asked, "You got something?"

"Yes," replied Dr. Hwang. "I found this neat gift at an herbal medicine shop."

Dr. Hwang gave the gift package to Dr. Nam, who read the description under his breath, "Facilitates the healthy circulation of qi through the meridians and improves blood flow to treat pain from stagnant blood …"

"Apparently it's good for after childbirth and things because it frees up blood flow," said Dr. Hwang.

Dr. Song took the package from Dr. Nam and considered it for a moment before she looked at Dr. Hwang. "For crying out loud, Dr. Hwang. We'll look ridiculous now that you've got this. Seriously, myrrh? It'll make our gifts look silly too. A gold ring, perfume, and myrrh on Christmas Eve? Heck, we're like the Three Wise Men here."

Dr. Hwang said, "At least Dr. Nam didn't get frankincense, he got perfume. They're two different things."

"Yeah, yeah. But the association is there, especially with myrrh on the gift list."

Sometimes, people become currency-goods themselves. If a power field compels it, they are bound to be sucked in. The trio turned themselves into a three-in-one biblical gift set and hurried up to Level 647.

None of them had ever been above Level 30 before. They commuted between the neighboring capital and Beanstalk every day, but this was their first time venturing up any higher than the research center. Following the visitor guide, they took the stairs beside the research center to Level 30 and walked to the nearest elevator stop. As they did not have commuter passes, they needed to get day passes, which were expensive at that time of year. The Christmas pass for groups of three covered their round trip to the hospital for the price of two, but they would need to stick together at all times on their way to the hospital and back.

In Beanstalk Tower, elevators did not take passengers from Level 1 to the top. If they did, they would need to stop at every floor, and a trip to the top might take a whole day. That was why a typical elevator line serviced only twenty or thirty floors. If the trio wanted to go up a hundred floors or more nonstop, they had to catch a long-distance elevator from a separate terminal. Long-distance express elevators bound for Level 500 passed through the Level 30 terminal. Christmas being right around the corner, the line for the express route was so long that the estimated wait time was an hour and a half, so the three of them crumpled up their queue-number tickets and decided to take an elevator to Level 60 instead. From there, they would find their way by consulting the elevator map in the visitor guide.

They were met with huge crowds in every corridor on Level 60. Lest they get swept away and lose each other, Dr. Nam held their group elevator pass above his head and took the lead. Stamped on the pass was a large, silver star that twinkled now and then as it caught the light of the city's brilliant displays.

After crossing a square on Level 60, they took route B77 up to Level 84. Then, after climbing two more floors by escalator, they walked five blocks toward the center of the building and caught a free ride up twelve floors using a department store elevator. But when they exited the department store, they realized that though they were on Level 98, they could not access elevator G15 from there, which forced them to go up another floor, take a roundabout route to the east, and climb back downstairs. They hopped on the G15 and got off at Level 129, just in time to catch the express from the long-distance terminal to Level 212. The problem was getting to Level 320.

"Transfer to Line L57 from Line L42 ..." Dr. Nam studied the map as he turned a corner, but glancing over his shoulder the other two were nowhere to be seen. As he began to debate whether to stand there or double back, thankfully his mobile rang. It was Dr. Song.

"Where are you? Why aren't you following?" Dr. Nam asked her.

"We were, but when we got closer it wasn't you. Every group of tourists is following someone holding a ticket above their heads."

After reuniting, they transferred three times to the Level 320 terminal and took a long-distance elevator to Level 427, which they had booked while on the move. As ten o'clock drew nearer the crowds thickened. It seemed as if half of

Beanstalk's population had spilled out into the walkways instead of staying put in their allotted spaces. Supposedly, every Christmas around ten Beanstalkians were trampled to death. The trio moved deeper into the center of the building and made two more transfers. By the time they pushed their way out of the elevator on Level 489, their faces had turned white.

"Hey, we're on Level 489," said Dr. Song, her face pale. "The dog lives on Level 487 at A57. That locus of power, Film Actor P. He might be out and about too. Should we go see him while we're here? Don't you want to see him in person?"

They changed course. It took them a full ten minutes to find a staircase, descend two floors, and locate A57. Although the area had a high concentration of power, it seemed to have low population density.

As they had expected, Film Actor P was taking a leisurely walk in a square near his home, reveling in the Christmas spirit. Strutting about and holding his head up so high he was in danger of falling backwards, Film Actor P carried himself like a veritable top dog. When he barked, he roared. He was surrounded by people who looked less like typical dog owners and more like bodyguards or secretaries. The sight of Film Actor P's staff sweating over every woof made the trio feel sorry for them.

"Did you hear that?" said Dr. Hwang. "He just barked, *compatriots*."

"Uh, you're kidding, right?" Dr. Nam asked.

"No, that's seriously what I heard."

It was hard to believe that Film Actor P's rise to power was entirely of his own making. What gave him power was the way his followers treated him and how they treated third parties. In that sense, A57 on Level 487 was very much a real power. The trio saw how Film Actor P's power warped the surrounding space, making passersby steer clear of a perfectly good path and edge around it.

Seeing that Dr. Song was right about A57 on Level 487, she had to be right about M225 on Level 193 too. This knowledge gave them a fresh surge of energy. Two floors down, they boarded Line E50 and went up to Level 537. They drew closer to rich neighborhoods the higher they went, so the corridors grew wider and the crowds thinner. Now and then they came across private elevators, the majority of which were "premium," "platinum," or "noblesse" lines that they couldn't take with their three-person Christmas pass. They had to walk a long way to find regular public transport. There was not much to see in these neighborhoods, affluent as they were. It was unusual, however, that one level was as high as four standard levels combined so that the walls looked especially tall, and cameras were installed across the ceiling. Some houses had left their gates ajar, offering glimpses of spacious private gardens over which an artificial sun shone down like real daylight.

Since every story in this rich district was so tall, one short-distance elevator serviced almost fifty levels—fifty when you counted by standard floors. But in reality, it only seemed to stop on about twenty floors. The trio transferred twice more and reached Level 632. They felt winded.

Dr. Song asked, "What altitude are we at?"

"I don't know, maybe two kilometers?" replied Dr. Nam.

They ascended two flights of stairs from the east end of the block. Development in the area was restricted to prevent an influx of people, but a long escalator, free of charge, ran up along glass windows like a moving observatory. The trio stepped onto it and looked out at the panoramic night view. Their faces had now turned sickly yellow. It was already 10.40 p.m.

They finally pushed through the hospital doors and found themselves standing in a garden where a great tree was planted. Goodness knows how it was carried up there, but what with the transportation cost and price of land, it was no doubt a criminally expensive tree, mused Dr. Hwang, whose thoughts were interrupted when a hospital staff member who had been staring at her asked in a concerned voice:

"Ma'am, do you need to see a doctor?"

"Oh, we're not here for me," replied Dr. Hwang.

Come to think of it, they made a strange group. One man and two women, all around the same age, visiting a postnatal unit at nearly eleven o'clock at night.

Silent night
Holy night
All is dark on this night

Down below Beanstalkians were heartily celebrating the birth of their savior, which is to say Santa Claus. But 649 levels above, the recovery room on the third floor of the hospital was silent to the point of being solemn.

Dr. Song asked, "Is it a boy or a girl?"

"It's a boy," the nurse replied.

Instead of angels, a nurse had heralded the birth of the baby.

The Three Wise Men—carrying the gold ring, perfume that was not frankincense, and myrrh—then followed the nurse's directions to the recovery room. Lights were switched off in all wards except the recovery room, creating the sad impression that they had come to a dingy stable no one ever visited. In fact, they had arrived at the reception room of a deluxe maternity suite, where everyone who needed to show up had already come and gone.

They knocked. No answer.

"Mr. Jung. Mrs. Jung. Are you asleep?"

They called a few more times but still no response. Dr. Song cracked open the door. The crime had already happened.

Silent night

Holy night

All is blood on L649 tonight

A cornered animal will turn around and bite. The three of them knew immediately what had cornered Professor Jung. It was the power of civilization, an invisible power. The force that makes you offer up your things to be stolen, without the powerful needing to threaten or order. The magic that makes you destroy political enemies and muzzle detractors, without the higher-ups having to handpick targets. The mysterious authority that makes the ruling body voluntarily rationalize and justify whatever claptrap comes tumbling out of the ruler's empty head. The power that is never interrogated no matter how dirty it plays because it is invisible.

A power field does not send assassins. It never bloodies its own hands, instead making its enemies draw their swords and end their own lives, political and social.

A little bit of civilization and barbarism go hand in hand in any society. When the power of the civilized world drives an individual to desperation, they resist by resorting to barbaric violence more often that you might expect. They delude themselves into thinking it is OK to do so. Professor Jung probably did too. But knowing that violence is the only means of resistance available to the powerless, the powers-that-be of civilization hate violence in the extreme. They punish it. Had Professor Jung not known that? But it would not have mattered anyway.

The bed, which should have been clean as a white canvas under the bright warm light, was covered in splashes of blood like an abstract expressionist painting. As if one stab had not been enough satisfaction, blood was splattered in every direction. The mother's blood flow had obviously been excellent. There would be no need for myrrh now.

The trio froze, unable to open the door all the way. Never in their wildest dreams could they have guessed that Professor Jung, who they thought knew nothing, had secretly drawn Beanstalk's power structure—including the dog—four times over.

Professor Jung turned towards the door, drenched in blood, his eyes vacant. He was still holding the knife.

"What brings you folks here at this hour?" Professor Jung's voice was casual. To the three of them, his question sounded like an accusation: did they come here suspecting something?

The jig was up. He was no longer human.

On that silent, holy night, a scream was heard on Level 649. Since screams were not out of place in a hospital at any time of the day, the sound itself did not alarm them. It was only when they saw people running that the situation finally sank in for the trio. They had seen something they should not have. Stepped into a place they should not have.

The trio took a deep breath and calmly walked through the hospital lobby. They crossed the garden like nothing had happened and slipped out the front door of the hospital. Faces pale again, they broke into a run, dashing towards the lower floors. Down the escalator with the panoramic view, back the way they came, changing elevators, hurtling down and down.

Professor Jung did not come after them. He stood rooted to the spot waiting for the police, or "security guards" in Beanstalk lingo. Yet the three recruits ran and ran. They kept pacing even inside elevators. As they passed the rich district with the high ceilings, the occasional tall shadow they saw seemed like the ghost of a giant robbed of his treasures. A ghost born out of the power field that included the dog, chasing them down the tower.

That was no delusion. They had to hurry. If they did not cross the border fast, they could be dragged into the murder case of M225's occupant, the hidden locus of power on Level 193, as key witnesses. It occurred to them as they ran that the occupant of A1 on Level 339.7 might hush up the case to ensure his reelection. But hushing up the case and stopping the investigation were two different things. Whether or not the murder was officially reported in the news, power would crank into motion. As far as they knew, in cases like this the mechanics of power was simple and clear. Eliminate everyone who knows of M225 on Level 193! Without of course getting blood on the hands of power!

Professor Jung, why did you do it when you know the drill!

However, such power did not work below the border. The trio transferred twelve times to go down—three times on long-distance elevators, nine on short-distance ones. It did not matter whether the nurses found the body or Professor Jung turned himself in; once security guards arrived on the scene and launched an investigation, and word reached the key members of power, Beanstalk's entire power field would immediately collapse and the Level 22 border would be sealed. How long before the border closed was anyone's guess. It hinged on when Professor Jung decided to talk, which could take anytime between ten minutes and a full day. Once a sleeping power field awoke, there was no avoiding or stopping it. Unless it devoured a suitable prey or met an even greater power field, it was beyond human control.

At last, the three recruits reached the Security Guardhouse zone. The power field did not seem to have collapsed yet. They passed through the departure gates with flushed faces. Just as they were entering the Demilitarized Zone on Level 21, where the shopping malls were, the power field came crashing down behind them, causing a flurry of activity among the security guards. In a matter of seconds, the departure gates were shut and immigration procedures for arrivals put on hold. The power field had spread open its jaws and bared its sharp fangs. The three of them instantly tensed up.

"Hey, you three!"

Hearing someone call out behind them, they wheeled round. It was a security guard calling her subordinates. Only then did they realize they had already exited the departure gates. They let out a sigh of relief.

It was better not to run now. Beanstalkian security guards didn't know their faces. The guards were not looking for people who knew the secret of M225 on Level 193, but were simply trying to prevent three key witnesses-cum-potential suspects of a murder case from leaving the building. As long as they did not act suspiciously, the guards had no reason to stop people who had crossed the border.

However, they were still on territory where Beanstalk wielded influence. To avoid looking like a trio, they descended the stairs one by one and managed to slip out of the vast twelve-story garden uninterrupted.

Dr. Song was first to exit the ground floor and tried to hail a cab on the boulevard right outside the building, but none stopped for her. She set out on foot. As she drew farther from Beanstalk Tower, she glanced back and saw a structure too big to fit inside her field of vision looming menacingly over people. She felt faint just by glimpsing it, a massiveness beyond common sense. Dr. Hwang soon came out of the building, but both of them pretended not to have seen each other.

As her tenseness subsided, Dr. Song noticed her feet were aching. She finally recalled the terrible scene at the hospital. *May Professor Jung be damned!* When Dr. Song was far enough from the entrance, she turned her trembling body and gazed up once more. A giant soaked in blood was staring down at her from the top of the building. On a closer look, it was just Santa Claus.

In Praise of Nature

The moment his reelection became official, the mayor launched a feasibility study on revamping the vertical transportation system of the city's outskirts. Of course, this was not the first time there had been talk of an upgrade. In a building such as Beanstalk with a resident population of 500,000, constructing more elevators was always a hot topic. Yet as transportation capacities increased, the number of users did as well. No matter how many elevators were added, traveling up and down 674 floors was always a hassle and people were always complaining. If someone actually solved this problem, they would surely—without needing to achieve anything else—stay in office until their dying day. Naturally, expanding the elevator service was a trump card that every mayoral candidate longed to play.

The issue had come under the spotlight once more because

vertical transportation companies were accused of being too cozy with politicians. When decisive evidence of collusion was found, the people who had a responsibility to watchdog the government were the first to start criticizing it. The city government promptly rounded up these critics and dug up any dirt it could on them. The government did not threaten the critics' freedom of expression, but it strictly enforced any unrelated regulations it could.

K had dirt on him. He probably had no more than other people, but K wasn't sure he had much less either. Although the government was yet to dig anything up on him, K had watched others go through the process. Sitting quietly in his corner, K observed that there was dirt to be found on everyone eventually. You mishandled business expenses, you dined with a student's parents before exams, or your registered address was different from your actual place of residence—one or two trivial but undeniable indiscretions were discovered without fail. All sorts of wrongdoings, which you otherwise would not have remembered until you were made to recall your lifetime of sins before the King of the Afterworld. The prospect of being placed beneath the guillotine of public scrutiny, like a fish to be sliced into sashimi, was a frightening one for K.

Once the obvious watchdogs over the government were quieted, other voices spoke up. Then, the security guards took the lead in digging up their dirt. As before, at no point was anyone's freedom of expression or freedom of assembly taken away. The rules were simply enforced a little more rigorously in other areas. The day after a massive protest took place at the square on Level 321, the people who had applied to use the space were arrested and interrogated by security guards on charges of violating the Inter-Floor Noise Control Act. A few writers who had made a speech mocking the government's ties to the vertical transport companies were accused of writing pornography and lost all future publication opportunities. The city government had not ordered these measures—someone with just enough power to do so had orchestrated them voluntarily.

Then, the BS Writers' Collective—locals sometimes referred to Beanstalk as "BS"—went on strike. Some writers declared they would stop publishing until the next election, but K continued to write. And that was exactly when he turned into a nature writer.

"Started extolling the beauty of Mother Nature, he did," said the editor-in-chief.

"No wonder K's style changed so much recently," said D.

"Yes. But the thing is, the man has terraphobia."

"Terraphobia?"

"It's been twenty-five years or so. Apparently, as a child he saw a terrorist bombing up close somewhere abroad. That's what made K such a die-hard realist writer if you ask me. But anyway, he's been terraphobic ever since. He can't go down to the ground floor. He's moved from one high rise to another until he ended up here in Beanstalk. I hear he used to have it pretty rough, what with an author's modest income and the high home prices. K's been on benefits ever since the city recognized his phobia as a disability. Some people suspect he's turned to nature writing because he might stop getting those benefits if he criticizes the government. But I don't think that's why—K earns a lot these days."

"I guess he does have a considerable following," said D.

"Of course he does. Each of his books sells around a hundred thousand copies in Beanstalk alone. The mayor didn't get a hundred thousand votes in the last election, so K's doing better than the mayor."

"True. But what's wrong with being terraphobic?"

"Because a guy who hasn't gone out of the building once for more than a decade is sitting around praising nature."

D was reminded of a work by K she had recently read. She did not remember finding any of it odd. D had even been touched by the story of a polar bear that, while foraging for food on ever thinning ice amid global warming, discovers the persistent chain of karma between itself and its prey, meditates for three days and three nights until it grasps the workings of the universe, and enters nirvana.

"Is it necessarily a problem that someone who hasn't been outdoors in a long time praises nature?" D asked.

The editor-in-chief replied, "For one, there's no authenticity. He's basically paraphrasing what he has read somewhere else, isn't he? Maybe that's why his writing has no *oomph*. Don't you agree?"

Thus D, under the editor-in-chief's orders, took on the job of once again trying to persuade K to write the realist fiction he used to.

K was sunbathing at a window-side resort in the southern

section of Level 410. D offered a standard greeting and began explaining the purpose of her visit, but before she could finish, K got up and disappeared into the pool.

Why is she bothering me when there's plenty of other people, K mused as he floated in the water, staring up at the ceiling. *Anyway, I can't write the stuff she wants me to write. I just can't.*

Still floating on his back, K shook his head. The cause of his reluctance was the villa in Frigiliana.

He called it a "villa," but it was not a very big house. Frigiliana was a small mountainside town on the southern coast of Spain. Often called "the white village," it was a Mediterranean-style town—its steep, narrow alleyways winding up a high hill lined with houses that had nothing in common except that they were all white. Many of them had a blue door or blue wooden windowsills, with nice little touches like flowerpots hanging on walls. Even the stone paving on the ground drew the eye. But the most impressive quality about Frigiliana was the weather. If you climbed the hill and looked south, the Mediterranean Sea lay in the distance, the horizon marking the beginning of an azure sky that stretched overhead and blanketed the whole town. It was a beautiful sight to behold. The crisp blue accentuated the white hue of the houses. In Frigiliana, what mattered was not owning a large house but a pretty one. There was no need for the former.

Of course, K had never been to Frigiliana himself. To get there, he would have to go down to the ground floor, fly to Madrid, take a train to Málaga, and then a bus to Nerja. From there, he would have to take another bus up a mountain road until the white houses appeared, sprinkled across the mountainside like perpetual snow. At least that was what he had heard from a former resident of Frigiliana.

It was horrible for K to even imagine the journey. Him, taking the train and the bus? Not to mention descending to the ground floor. He could go almost nowhere unless he was traveling by helicopter. Even that felt unsafe after Cosmomafia shot down a commercial airplane. Transportation methods were no longer purely for transportation. If K went anywhere below Level 50, where the horizon encroached up to a considerable height in his field of vision, his breath quickened out of inexplicable fear. Below Level 30, all rational thought was numbed by a delusion so ridiculous that K himself was baffled by it: the image of numberless corpses punching through the ground and sitting up, every head swiveling towards him. In vain, K would try to compose himself by thinking again and again that such a vision was irrational, but he often wound up in a panic attack that left him desperately in need of immediate help. K never stopped seeing a shrink about this because he wanted to visit Frigiliana, but his terraphobia was unshakeable no matter what he did. It was infuriating.

That villa was a gesture of goodwill by someone whose name he could not disclose. It was clearly meant as a bribe, and the terms expected in return were explicit. Yet when K was first introduced to the villa, he thought his briber was joking—the southern coast of Spain was as inaccessible to him as a cake in a painting. But his opinion changed when he saw the perk that came with the house.

The perk was a robot. Not an overly sophisticated or powerful one. It didn't even have that many functions; it simply moved about the house as it was directed and picked up items with its crude arms. It was incapable of going outside the house. The machine simply looked like what we might call a robot. Still, it was enough for K. To be precise, what really captivated him was not the robot itself, but the view captured by its powerful camera. Through the robot, K could move about the house and gaze out the windows as if he lived there. The first time he tried looking out of one through the robot's eyes, he instantly fell head over heels for the picturesque hilltop town near the Mediterranean.

K accepted the gift without thinking. The eagerness of his acceptance surprised even his benefactor. This was the biggest piece of dirt on K. One he could not and did not want to return. The house in Frigiliana was technically not owned by him, only the robot was, and on paper K was renting the robot from the owner. Despite these precautions, it was not a perfect ruse. Anyone could see through it if they tried hard enough.

The house contained another trap that would allow anyone to frame K as an even bigger scumbag if they wanted: Rosa, the girl who regularly came to keep the robot in good repair and clean the house.

Rosa's first visit was well over a month after K was gifted the house, so he did not know about her in the beginning. For her work, Rosa received a pretty good sum. Too good, in fact, for visiting only twice a month. K was startled when he later found out. He told the owner that he would rather pay the girl's wages himself, but the owner firmly declined, telling

K not to worry—the money was meant as a sort of scholarship for a promising robotics student. Seeing it was for a charitable purpose, K pressed the matter no further.

In retrospect, the whole business seemed like the house owner's scheme. Of course, Rosa truly did nothing other than robot maintenance and housekeeping, but she pocketed an excessively big check and she was excessively good-looking. If anyone who harbored bad intentions found out about her, they had enough fodder to spread outlandish rumors. "What on earth could she be up to? She earns more working twice a month than a low-level public servant does working full-time." That question alone could wreak damage.

The thought made K feel cheated. But he liked Rosa—she was a good kid, hardworking. She never broke a promise or was late, nor did she head out early. Not once did she bring her friends over to throw a party or carelessly leave her things around. The house was always clean and the robot in excellent condition. Rosa was like that. She was someone who, in her own way, made the world a better place to live. K did not wish to cut Rosa off from her "scholarship."

After changing into her swimsuit, D returned to the pool and jumped in, at which K slowly moved his limbs and swam out. He did not want to bother answering her inevitable question. Or bother thinking about anything at all.

"Please, sir," said D. "For an artist of your stature, there's no reason why you should be so hesitant. Your readership isn't limited to Beanstalk. I'm not sure what's holding you back from writing hard-hitting fiction again. Is something else worrying you?"

It was not such a simple matter. It was too complicated to

explain, too easy to create misunderstanding. Not saying anything would be the best choice. Pure intentions and goodwill are impossible to fully explain in words. The more one tried, the more one felt like a swindler. K gave no answer. D proceeded to follow him around, persistently trying to persuade him.

K asked, "Where are you going to follow me to?"

"To the end."

"This is the men's changing room."

"I can wait."

"Do you think I'll come out through here if you wait? I'd take the exit leading outside. And don't you need to change?"

He was right. This would not do.

"Then I'll quickly get changed and wait for you at the other exit. Please don't leave first."

When D rushed away to get changed, K got back into the water. Since K never showed up despite a long wait, D lamented that she must have missed him and went home.

D told the editor-in-chief what had happened as soon as she got to work the next morning.

The editor-in-chief snapped, "You're not very bright, are you?"

Only then did D realize, to her outrage, that she had been duped. She phoned K immediately and demanded to know how he could do such a thing. K answered in mock surprise, "Oh, I didn't leave. I went outside and waited for a long time, but you didn't come out. I figured you must've left and went on my way. Didn't you leave first?"

He was lying, obviously.

But she could not hate him. She had never thought of K as a mercenary or morally reprehensible writer. Sure, you may be able to dig up a little dirt on him, but he was an upright and honorable man. D knew that K could hurl a gloriously foul insult when the situation called for it, but he also had enough self-control to stop himself from insulting the wrong person.

D did not wish to press K, she was just frustrated. She supposed he must be holding his sharp tongue for a good reason, and she doubted he would keep his silence forever. When D told him as much, K said, "So you're saying I have a foul mouth? Looking for a good cusser, are you?"

"No, you know that's not what I mean." D politely pleaded with him again, "Sir, you're the only one who can speak up."

"Nonsense. There are plenty of other folks. Why me?"

However, K eventually relented at D's tireless persuasion. "I'll write something up and send it to you. Use it if it's any good or else throw it out. And don't bring this up with me ever again."

Two months later, K sent D a manuscript as promised. Eagerly, she began to read in silence but after reading the first few lines, she scowled. The editor-in-chief asked, "What's wrong? Is it bad?"

"No, I've only read ten lines so I'm not sure yet," replied D.

"Is it weird from the beginning then?"

"It's about the beauty of nature again."

"Again?"

One could not say it was wrong of K to write about a round

world while living trapped in a square one. Nor could one say K was a traitor for waxing lyrical about the beauty of nature like a fishing enthusiast might do when he used to capture the dark underbelly of society with uncomfortably trenchant and raw language. Even when parts of the world were on the brink of devastating war, someone had to keep watching climate change trends, someone had to peer at the seismometer all night long. The world was like that. But no matter how much D thought about it, that person did not have to be K.

"What should I do, chief?" asked D.

"Well. You should give it a read anyway. If it turns out to be passable, salvage what you can. This is what you signed up for."

Sitting up straight in her seat, D resumed reading the manuscript calmly, with neither anticipation nor prejudice. She phoned K before she finished two pages.

"Sir, did you really write this?"

"What is it now? Why are you yelling at me?"

"I'm sorry. But there are a lot of odd sentences."

"That's because I rushed through it. It's only the first draft."

D read five more pages and called K again.

"Sir, does someone have something on you?"

"What is it this time?"

"You never used to indulge in bland writing like this. There isn't even a narrative arc."

"That's because I'm old. I like it uneventful these days."

After he hung up, K stared at his monitor for a long time, dumbstruck.

My writing is bland?

He was shaken. He had not received such feedback in fifteen years. Although K had written bland and boring stuff in that time, such manuscripts were not shared with other people. The issue was not that his writing had become bland. There was no need to worry about producing mediocre works as long as his eye for filtering them out stayed sharp—the manuscripts simply needed to be destroyed before they were shown to anyone. But if he had lost that eye, K was finished.

The thought angered him. It was all Frigiliana's fault. And Rosa's. K had forced himself to write something he had little desire to write about and, as a result, mistaken the usual agony of creative writing for the quality of the work. He had expected the work to be good because it had been such a pain to write, and the process had dulled his writerly eye. But once K calmed down and thought things over, he admitted Frigiliana and Rosa were not really responsible. It had clearly been *his* choice to write the work. K had blamed Rosa for something he would have written anyway.

K looked at the Frigiliana house in his monitor. It was the third Saturday of the month, the day when Rosa visited. He would have to wait a long time to see her, as it was still early morning in Spain. The sky was already a clear blue. The house was covered in light dust but cozy all the same. Still, none of that registered with him.

He phoned D and calmly said, "I'm going to send you a rewrite so please see to it that the thing in your hands is destroyed. Can I trust you to ensure that nobody else reads that?"

"Yes, sir!" D answered and loudly ripped his story to pieces before K even put down his receiver.

K shouted indignantly, "That's a bit harsh!"

K sat down and resolved to write the masterpiece of his lifetime. But nothing came to mind. He perused his bookshelf for inspiration. Something about the shelf bothered him. He took out every single book and grouped them by color and size. He realized it was a crazy thing to do only when he had finished. By the time K reorganized his shelf by theme and author, it was long past sundown.

K extracted the ideas from his head, one by one. There was a story latched onto each idea. Some ideas had fairly long stories attached to them; others only had the events happening immediately before and after. No idea came with a complete story. There would be no need for writers if such a thing existed.

Some fledgling stories served as links between isolated ideas. That was how sizable lumps of stories often formed effortlessly in K's head over time. He peered inside his own head: three lumps floated about, each large enough to be written up right away. One of them had such near-perfect form that a full story might come tumbling out as soon as his fingers touched the keyboard.

The Mayor and the Elevator! This story even came with a title, but it was not the right time to write it. K had to bide his time until there was a change of government, when all relevant parties had stepped down from office. Only then, keeping his tone calmly retrospective, could he raise his regretful voice on the injustices that had dominated the era.

Damn it! I'd have to live for a long time!

K considered writing about the dog on Level 487 instead, with the title "The Dog and the Elevator."

At least dogs have shorter lifespans.

He looked at his computer monitor. Rosa was due to appear soon. She always arrived fifteen minutes earlier than the appointed time. In itself, Rosa turning up fifteen minutes early did not necessarily indicate she was a hard worker because the buses traversed the town at fixed intervals. But it was better than her being late fifteen minutes every time. No, it made a huge difference to K. He moved the robot with his mouse. The robot waved. There was a two-second lag. Rosa smiled at the camera. That was all.

K drove the robot to the window which, according to the owner, offered the best view in all of Frigiliana. He was glued to the window, gazing up at the blue sky, when Rosa came over and wiped the glass. The sky grew a little cleaner. She was someone whom you could not help but root for. Justice was meaningless if it couldn't make kids like Rosa happy.

Looking back at the sky, K felt as though his heart was clearing. He could not bear the idea that people could see these clear and simple, innocent things as smelly and dirty and deceitful. It was a while before Rosa finished cleaning and went home. He watched her go in silence. Even the way she walked was upright. He concluded that nature was the answer after all.

Yes. There's nothing wrong with nature. It's the best thing we have! Humans can't live away from it, anyway.

K stretched his hands over the keyboard. After typing and deleting a few words, he began to write something at last. He typed late into the night without taking a break. He had a good feeling.

But turmoil stirred inside K again by the time he wrapped up his work and climbed into bed. The stories he had carefully kept buried in a corner of his heart these past five months since the day the mayor was re-elected now filled his mind. K pulled the blanket up to his nostrils and considered "The Mayor and the Elevator." It was a gripping idea—uncontrived stories linking smaller ideas with such cohesiveness that if he just nailed the first sentence, the rest would follow effortlessly. The narrative in his mind was perfect, so much so that he could just take the characters, style, and themes and use them without making any adjustments. It was beyond brainstorming; it was a fully formed brainchild. Encountering such a complete story was rare.

K wrote the whole story in his head as he lay there. He was satisfied. Then, he sat bolt upright, only to lie back down again. He stared wide-eyed at the ceiling. No—nature was always the answer. No matter how K looked at it, now was not the time for denunciation. Sleep washed over him.

D received a manuscript from K a month later. It was the first half of a story about nature.

… *In the beginning, there was a tree. The notion of gods had yet to exist as it was long before the advent of humans. Sky, earth, sea, grass, and forest were all there was. This tree was the god of trees, the largest tree in the world. It put down its roots and* lived there for 5,500 years. It had such lush, green foliage. It looked around and felt proud, rewarded, and moved to see that no other tree had carried leaves up to greater heights. But when it awoke after eons of slumber and revealed itself to the world again, not a trace of its lush foliage remained. Only its enormous trunk, tissue replaced by minerals, rested deep beneath the ground, looking just as it had when it was alive.

The tree was the most colossal organism ever found by humans. The planet's largest organism was not one of the moving life forms with bones or flesh, such as whales, dinosaurs, elephants, or giant squids. Those moving organisms that had boastfully compared themselves with other beings to confirm their enormous size each day were reduced to trivial creatures beside the colossal, primordial god that had resurfaced at last.

Two hundred and seventy-nine meters. The excavation team was aghast. A gargantuan tree whose full length they failed to uncover though they dug, dug, and dug. It was buried in a reclining position, suggesting it had fallen at some point. But the moment the excavation team laid eyes on the dead body of this great being, which had stood proud without relying on another soul for 5,500 years, they felt something ignite inside them, something they had carried deep inside their genes for a long, long time: veneration for a life by a life. Tears welled in their eyes …

How disappointing. Escapism in the present climate? And by K of all people. D thought she had better go and see him in person. When she phoned to ask if K could spare her some time, he invited her to his place—a highly unusual event.

When D arrived at K's home, he called her over to his

workroom and began in a serious tone, "There's a place called Frigiliana. In southern Spain."

"I know that area. How do you know about it, sir?"

"You've been there?"

"Yes. My dad used to have a villa on Torrox Beach, near Nerja. It's a popular destination for the British and Germans. I've seen northern Europeans there in mid-winter walk around in short sleeves and short trousers. Lots of them buy houses and settle there after retiring. My dad was a realtor there for British clients, you see. But how do you know about that place? Presumably you've never been there."

K nodded and came clean about everything that had been plaguing him for months. The villa, the robot, even Rosa. D was shocked by his story. Though she did not show it, she was frankly disappointed. She carefully hid her thoughts as she told K, "I understand where you're coming from. It sounds like a delicate situation."

K gave no response. D asked, "By the way, what did they ask from you in return? They must've wanted something if they gave you such a pricey gift." Her tone was accusing.

"Well, that's the thing, it was nothing big. They wanted me to connect someone to a publisher."

D was taken aback. Her stomach squirmed uncomfortably. In Beanstalk, where wages were high but jobs scarce, getting work as a foreigner was harder than plucking a star from the heavens. She remembered telling her friends she was going to work for a book publisher in Beanstalk and how they had teased, "Who hooked you up?" Her dad had, of course. D was not so naive as to be unaware of that. With clients in the

Beanstalk City Council as well as City Hall, her dad was a realtor in rather high demand. She was certain he had connections in the publishing industry too. *Hang on, did that mean …?*

"Um, sir, is there by any chance …"

"Yes, it was him. Your old man. You get the picture now, right? He roped me in with the villa, but returning it won't undo what's been done. The bottom line is that this could look quite scandalous."

Finally, D understood why the editor-in-chief had assigned an important writer like K to a rookie editor like her. The editor-in-chief must be furious with K and maybe with her as well. From that point on, she would find it very awkward to face K. Interacting with her boss would be just as awkward.

She went back to the office to re-read K's manuscript, more attentively this time. Then, D made up her mind. *Yes, there's nothing wrong with nature! As long as the writing is good. I wonder when he'll finish the second half.*

… Their original plan was to build a resort. The largest in the world. But as they drilled into the earth to create an immense underground space, they encountered an unexpected obstacle. It was a long, round rock. They could not drill down any further unless they broke the rock. It was bizarre—they had never seen such a long and round rock. They had never even heard of one like it. Before they broke the rock, they had to check the rest of it, which was buried in the ground.

They drilled a nearby area. The rock turned out to be cylindri-

cal, its shape growing more evident the more they drilled. Who had buried such a thing? There was no way to know. Nevertheless, they had to find out where this cylinder ended. They drove a metal bar into the ground at a point thirty meters away. It hit the rock. They drove in another bar fifty meters away. It hit the rock again. They did the same thing seventy, ninety, and finally a hundred and eight meters away before they found one end of the rock. It was much longer than they had expected. The other direction was even longer.

What on earth is it?

No one knew. A geological survey team was eventually sent in. It concluded that an extremely hard stone pillar was stuck between two large rocks.

Is this possible? Who could've made something like that? We're not sure. What's more intriguing is that it's at least 800 million years old. 800 million? Who could've possibly built such a round stone pillar 800 million years ago?

All manner of excavation experts offered their views, and soon, the rock's true identity was uncovered. It was a tree. The materials making up its tissue had been incrementally replaced by minerals, until it had turned into a fossil that looked just like the titanic tree it had been in life. They had dug up the grave of a god …

… The tree was lost in thought. It recalled the long, resplendent summer. During frequent rains and wet winds, its roots squeezed the earth with a mighty grip and sucked in water and the heat of life at once. That vital heat travelled up its vast trunk, through the network of veins spread throughout its body, reaching the topmost branch in one, sweeping ascent.

The tree grew taller in the scorching sun, and its trunk toughened in storms. It thought its first thought when it turned 2,200 years old and heard its first sound at 3,200. It could faintly make out the beating of the earth's great heart, the sound pulsing up the tree's roots. The tree did not have a heart. So, it listened closely to hear the sound. It gripped the earth a little tighter.

The tree became a god at 4,200 years old. At 4,900, it heard the other trees speak. By 5,250, it had learned to talk by shaking its roots. Conversation began, the world opened. The sound of conversing trees filled the earth. Trees seized sounds.

Did you hear? Hear what? Just now? That boom. I did. Is the earth angry? No, the earth is gentle. Not always. Well it is now. It's me. What do you mean? It's where I am. What about it? The sound came from here. Really? Really? Over there? Is the earth angry? No. Then why? The earth is gentle. What kind of sound is it? A boom. What boomed? Something big. Did the earth explode? The earth was gentle. What boomed then? It crashed. What did? Another earth. Another earth? Yes, it wasn't ours. There is another earth? It flew here. From where? I don't know. Did it explode? No, it crashed. With our earth? Yes. Is it very big? It's small. Smaller than our earth? Much smaller. Why is it so loud, then? It has no heart. You mean the earth that flew here? Yes. Maybe it's dead. What does that mean?

Did you hear that? What? That boom. Who heard? Me. The you from just now? No, another me. Did the sound come from where you are? Yes. Really? Really? Another crash? Yes. By another earth? Yes. Does it also have no heart? No. Is it dead? Must be. Why would a dead earth … Why would it come flying, you mean? Yes. I don't know. Does anyone know? No. No. No. Me neither. No one does. No one knows apparently. How far away *are we? I'm close. Not me. Me neither. I'm not sure. How big is this earth? I don't know. Me neither. Me neither ...*

Someone had fallen to their death from a north-side window on Level 197. The incident had happened in the vertical transportation system redevelopment zone—the deceased had been one of the protesters occupying the area. On the tenth night of the sit-in, security guards had gone in to suppress the protest, and the resulting struggle had led to the accident.

However it had happened, any security operation resulting in someone's death was a failure in K's opinion. He could not see any room for excuses but no one from the city government came forward to take responsibility.

It saddened him. He gazed at Frigiliana as seen by the robot on his computer screen, before closing the program and deleting the robot user verification plugin, control software, and video receiver. Then, K finished the rest of his manuscript and sent it to D.

... Dead earths kept flying in from somewhere. The trees knew very well how enormous the earth in their grasp was. They believed it to be the entire universe. But the dead earths shooting in from outside changed their minds. Another world lay outside theirs. A world of small earths with no hearts.

The ground resounded with increasing frequency. Crashes occurred more often. The trees assiduously clasped the earth. Constant whispers reached deep into the ground.

It's going to crack at this rate. You mean our earth? Yes. There was another crash. A dead earth? Yes, it has no heart. A small earth. Yes, they keep coming.

Winter arrived. One that was as long as the resplendent summer. Asteroids knocked tirelessly on the planet. Then, the atmosphere grew murky until it veiled the sun completely. Leaves fell one by one. The great tree was stunned. How could so many leaves rain down in so few days? A heap had formed atop the tree's roots. Don't fall. The tree clutched its roots tightly each time a leaf hanging precariously at the tip of its branches gave up and plummeted, toward the frozen earth two hundred meters below. Deep screams quaked the earth.

I'm sorry. It's my fault.

But the tree was not to blame for the onset of winter, nor for the dying leaves. What did it mean to die? The tree had already become a god one thousand years ago. It loosened its roots and meditated…

As she always did, Rosa arrived at the house at 3.45 p.m. that Saturday. The robot was not moving, but that was not unusual. Since its operator lived on the other side of the planet, the robot also lived in an opposite time zone. She checked over the robot, cleaned the house, and made sure the robot was fully charged before she went home.

Rosa visited the robot two weeks later at the same time. It was still not moving. She did a thorough inspection but found nothing wrong. She finished cleaning, checked the battery again, and went home. Suspecting something was amiss, Rosa looked in on the robot the next day and found it exactly as it had been, immobile, staring blankly up at the sky.

TOWER

Two days later, she appeared with a blanket and change of clothes and spent the night beside the robot. It did not make a noise throughout the whole night. Not one motor whirred, not one lens shifted.

Is it dead?

Rosa recalled everything she knew about robots as she examined it. But it was functioning normally.

Did its soul leave?

Robots obviously did not have souls. Rosa thought of the robot's operator who, she had heard, lived halfway across the world. She had never met them or spoken to them. She didn't know their name, age, gender, or race. They were simply someone who waved the robot's arm at her when she stepped into the house, who, when she looked back as she walked down the hill after work, poked the robot's head out the window to watch her go. *They* were the robot's soul.

Did it really die?

… A thick blanket of snow blossoms covered the now leafless branches. The great tree curled up its roots in the face of a cold it had never felt before, gripping the earth without meaning to speak. The other trees recognized its voice.

It's the tree that's been silent. It's alive. It is. What did I tell you? It didn't die. It will soon. We all will. We don't have leaves. Our branches are broken. Something is piled on them. They feel so heavy. Our bodies are heavy. We're going to die soon. But what's dying?

The great tree said nothing as it listened to the other trees talk. It could hear better when it stayed quiet and loosened its roots.

It listened to the other trees for two decades without uttering a single word. Then one day, at last, it gripped the earth with all its might.

What can we do to make summer come?

It was a long sentence. A deep rumble burrowed into the earth. The question posed by the tree traveled through the mantle beneath the crust, spreading to every tree around the world. No one answered.

Can we stop heartless earths from falling on our earth?

Another long sentence reverberated across the earth. The trees heard that lingering, beautiful echo and felt a thrill. Though the trees lacked hearts themselves, they felt a hopeful thump-thump-thump in their bosoms.

Are there enough of us? Yes? Everyone who can, make noise.

All the enlightened trees in the world tightened their roots and squeezed. The tree heard them. There were a lot of them. Countless. The tree had not known the world hosted such a great number of trees. Their regular clenching and unclenching of the earth sounded like thunderous heartbeats. It was as if the earth had gained another heart.

If there were this many trees that knew how to produce sound, there would be many more that only knew how to listen, and many times more that did not know how to listen. Taking into account the immature trees and insentient trees, the number of trees on earth soared well beyond the tree's imagination.

I see now that we've already filled the world. We're not alone, we are a forest.

At those words, the earth's second heart pounded fiercely.

Listen, trees! Since we're occupying the whole world, couldn't we catch every heartless earth before they reach our earth? I don't know how high up the other world is, but if we grow a little more, couldn't we fill the skies too? Wouldn't summer return if the heartless earths stopped hitting our earth?

The sentences flowed like song, pumping the heart. The earth sent up the heat of life to its new heart. Absorbing that heat, the trees rose higher and higher. Forests mushroomed toward the heavens from a snowy, frozen land that had nothing left but its blizzards. Two centuries under the snow. Trees that had become gods kept growing without a single leaf. Their goal was to pierce the sky. They had never seen it. They did not know how high it was. Yet 27.4 billion towering trees enveloped the earth and sang, yearning to reach the sun someday, to have summer shine down on their heads in all its glory. A booming, simple song not unlike a beating heart rang out without a day of rest.

Yet the winter was long. The snow blossoms piled on branches grew unbearably heavy. One by one the trees lost their lives. They were dying. The second heart's vigor waned. Finally, the day came when all life expired. Only one heart remained in the earth ...

I stopped writing at this point and wondered what on earth I was doing. This was no time to elegize about trees. People are born and die every second, but that doesn't make the weight of death any lighter. This cruel winter brought on by state power isn't any less cold for having crushed just one life, just one truth.

The public prosecutor's office has cleared the security guards of all accountability. But it launched a new investigation whenever new evidence emerged. It separated the new evidence from the rest of the case and investigated only those parts of the incident further. The people whose job it is to make Beanstalk a beautiful place said that, while they deeply regretted the death, they didn't think any of the people in charge were to blame. I hadn't turned on the news so I could listen to this bullshit.

If the world that the deceased saw before they died was full of despair and hatred and sorrow, every single person in charge is to blame. There used to be a time when nature was responsible for making the world beautiful. A world where the splendor of Mother Nature covered all the dirt and filth of humanity. An age when you could turn your back on injustice and say, "My humble person has the leisure to elegize about trees," and as the refrain of a Joseon-dynasty song goes, "This too is thanks to His Majesty's grace."

Why yes! This too is thanks to His Excellency the mayor. But a person had clung to Level 197 for dear life, and the truth hid behind a black veil, offering only tantalizing glimpses of itself. Who the blazes should we thank for that? How strange that supposedly no one erred when clearly someone did. Perhaps that someone was me. Yes, that must be it. Everything turns out to be my fault.

I dug out and read a manuscript I wrote at twenty-eight. I was quite the discontented youth. Nothing seemed right to me. Everything was the establishment's fault. I criticized and attacked it. "Have passion and be proactive, challenge yourself," people said. I asked them, "Have you built a world that can reward my passion and hard work?" I questioned everything with defiance.

But now I belonged to the establishment. If the world still wasn't beautiful after twenty years, I was in no position to criticize anyone. The fault was mine. I was guilty. I was the one re-

sponsible for the world not being beautiful. I resolved to put aside my many pleasures and write that …

What followed were not words. They were insults. For better or for worse, the publisher daringly printed them verbatim.

"You lot are crazy," K said.

"Why, thank you," D replied, drawing a resigned chuckle from K.

Of course, the government did not stifle art or the freedom of expression; it only dug up the dirt on K—Frigiliana, Rosa, the bribe defying common sense, and much more. There was more dirt on K than expected. His acquaintances were astounded, as was K himself.

"I told you I didn't want to do it," said K.

"Well, I didn't know things were *this* bad. I'd always thought of you as a man of honor. I'm shocked," said D.

Difficult days began for D and K both. A beautiful world remained elusive.

K thought of Rosa at times. Her scholarship money must have been rescinded. He supposed she would be doing well for herself, wherever she was, whatever she was doing. But sometimes, he worried that that might not be the case.

One day, seventeen years later, K felt a sudden urge to see Frigiliana. He was part curious and part concerned the town had turned into a kitschy tourist attraction. However, his terraphobia had not improved one bit. If anything, he was close to developing a phobia of public squares. His dream of visiting the town in person looked like it would never come true.

K searched the Internet, thinking he could at least find some pictures of the town, and fortunately, Frigiliana didn't seem to have become a tourist trap yet. He found a picture of the house his robot used to live in. K had heard that a retired British couple stayed there for half the year, but that was twelve years ago so he had no idea who lived there now. The exterior of the house, at least, seemed to have changed very little from seventeen years ago.

Well into his web surfing, he stumbled on a strange headline: BRAIN DEAD ROBOT IN FRIGILIANA. LOOKING FOR LOST SOUL.

K thought it was an advertisement, but when he read on it turned out to be something altogether different. It was written by Rosa. He clicked on a link which contained instructions in English, Chinese, and Spanish on how to access the soul again and downloaded the required program. After struggling to remember his password for a long time, K managed to reconnect to the robot. This took him one full day.

The robot opened its eyes. The scenery caught on its camera was relayed to K's computer screen. The place looked familiar. A vista of Frigiliana, just as he had last seen it. He operated the robot relying on his hazy memory. The wheels, the camera, they were all the same. The robot was in excellent condition, even after seventeen years. He looked around the house. No one was there. But the house was clean, without a speck of dust in sight.

It was Saturday night, Saturday afternoon in Frigiliana

time. At 3.45 p.m., Rosa opened the door and walked in as she always used to. She was astonished to see that the robot had shifted to another spot on its own. She peered into the camera.

K looked at Rosa's face, which now filled his screen. He moved his mouse to control the robot. It waved. There was a two-second lag, just as there had been seventeen years ago. Rosa, now approaching middle age, smiled back at the robot.

From one life to another. From a living soul to another.

It doesn't matter who you are. So long as you are alive, as you are now.

Hello! How have you been?

That was what Rosa's smile meant. That was all.

K rummaged through his memories. One thing was for certain. He could not recall ever seeing such a radiant smile.

Taklamakan Misdelivery

Those words jogged Eunsoo's memory of Minso. They were both twenty-five then, and Minso was her first love. Someone special from long ago. A kind, smart boy. Five years ago, in fact—she had drifted away from him after she moved to Beanstalk. Remembering him still brought a smile to Eunsoo's lips, but she had not bothered to reach out to him in a very long time.

First loves were better left in the past. Even if she had gone to the trouble of seeking him out, she felt she would have been disappointed. Back then, she was a kid who knew nothing about the real world, as was Minso. A quick look through their old photos would confirm that. Maybe she didn't even have to look at the photos; Minso would no doubt be pictured sporting what now seemed like an old-fashioned hairstyle, an old-fashioned outfit, and a boyish grin. Beaming artlessly. Eunsoo found herself missing that artless grin.

"How do you know Minso?" she asked.

Byungsoo looked at her and continued uncertainly, "I'm not sure if I can say I *know* him. It's a long story. Do you have a moment?"

"How long do you need?"

"Maybe five minutes? Ten?"

Eunsoo hesitated for a second, but then led Byungsoo to the breakroom.

"Could you wait here?" she asked. "I just have to wrap up what I was doing, I'll be right back." Eunsoo's heart pounded. How did she forget about Minso? They may have drifted apart, but how could she have forgotten the boy?

Her memory skipped back to the day she moved into Beanstalk Tower five years ago. It had been a warm day in May, the height of spring. The day she crossed the Beanstalk national border for the first time, having landed an internship at Level 599. Minso was walking behind her, pulling her luggage. They stopped before the crosswalk.

"You should go now," said Eunsoo.

But Minso insisted, "I'll walk you to the border."

"Yeah?"

Minso gazed at her. Unable to meet his eyes, she looked down at her toes without saying anything.

Minso said he felt like this would be it, once they said goodbye.

"You know that's not going to happen," said Eunsoo.

The cars stopped. Eunsoo and Minso had barely reached the middle of the crosswalk when the green light began flashing, rushing them. Slowly, Minso trailed after Eunsoo.

"Hurry!" she pressed. "Or you'll get hit!"

"OK."

She grew frustrated watching Minso feebly cross the road.

"I'm not going far away. I'll be here. Just twenty minutes away."

"You won't be able to leave often."

"I got in. I might as well work hard."

"You won't even get to call."

"Like I said, it's for security reasons."

"What security bans interns from calls and emails?"

"Look, Minso, that's the way things are here. Everyone accepts that. They can teach the business to even interns *because* the security is so tight. Otherwise, they'd never teach me. I'd rather hang out with you, but think of my age—if I did everything I wanted, when would I ever get anywhere?"

"A year's still too long."

"You were in the army for two years."

"I didn't sign up for it."

"Do you think I'm going because I want to?"

But the truth was, she did want to go—badly. E & K was the best satellite design firm in the world. Budding designers like Eunsoo would kill to work there.

"Then don't go," said Minso.

"Minso, I told you. In the satellite biz, so long as you have the name E & K on your resume, you'll get hired even if you forgot to write your own name."

"Even if all you do at E & K is make copies?"

"Of course! Even if all I do is make coffee the E & K way."

Recalling these old memories, Eunsoo hastily wrapped up

her work and hurried back to the breakroom. As soon as she sat down with Byungsoo, she casually asked what she had been dying to know. "So, what's Minso up to these days?"

Byungsoo's face suddenly darkened. He said, in what sounded like a rehearsed tone, "He's gone missing. In the Taklamakan Desert. For the past eight hours."

"The desert?"

"His jet was shot down. The military is tracking him down right now."

Was he asleep or unconscious? Dreams kept mingling with reality. Minso knew he was in a barren desert, but when he opened his eyes, he saw a long stretch of shade. His eyes followed the shade and found Beanstalk. The building was eroding before him, raising a cloud of sand. No, that was not possible. It must be an illusion.

In Minso's eyes, Beanstalk was another Tower of Babel—a city of hubris. He hated that Eunsoo had found a job there. It was only an internship, but Eunsoo seemed to think moving into Beanstalk would make all her dreams come true.

It would not. Beanstalk was not welcoming to unestablished migrant workers like Eunsoo. Despite sitting on foreign territory, Beanstalk denied visa-free entry to even that foreign territory's citizens.

Minso thought back to that day five years ago, the last time he saw Eunsoo. They exited the subway and walked one block before they reached the crosswalk at Beanstalk Intersection. Cars stopped and the lights changed. They had barely reached the middle of the crosswalk when the green light began flashing, rushing them. Minso felt a stab of frustration.

Eunsoo did not need to be rushed; she would be leaving soon anyway. She would cross that border without hesitation, maintaining her pace. Eunsoo was that kind of girl. Once she set her mind on something, she did it.

You think you're the only one who's like that, Eunsoo? I'm determined too.

Minso was suddenly resentful. Eunsoo's ultimatum was unfair. She had left him no choice, having already decided to break up with him.

Eunsoo had said, "If you don't like our arrangement, we'll just have to break up."

But even if he went along with the arrangement, he knew they would break up eventually. Letting Eunsoo go with a smile was the same as breaking up for him. That place was going to wear her down. The thought of sending Eunsoo into that devil's lair! He remembered looking up as Beanstalk Tower loomed before him, too tall for him to see to the top. He had known Beanstalk was not pure evil, yet it somehow irked him. An internationally accepted sovereign state despite its territory being a mere building. A 674-story building that drew a strict border between itself and where he lived, despite only being a twenty-minute bus ride away. A people that bristled when told they live in a modern-day Tower of Babel.

"What conceited bastards, right?"

Eunsoo nodded awkwardly at Minso's words.

Minso looked up at the sky amid his flashbacks. The sun was already high above the horizon. He must have broken his leg. Or had he hurt his neck? He could not move at all. Nor could he see any shade to rest under.

He had become a pilot for that very same nation of bastards and was returning from a bombing mission when he was struck by a surface-to-air missile. If the enemy found him first, he would be in deep trouble. Unfortunately, the odds of being found by the Beanstalk Defense Forces first seemed close to zero. Since the main bulk of the Defense Forces were stationed on Level 24 of Beanstalk, the point of his crash was probably closer to enemy lines than Beanstalkian forces.

I sure am one unlucky bastard.

He only had six months left of service. He had planned to spend two of those months on vacation. Had he made it through that half a year, he would have obtained Beanstalkian citizenship. After enduring four long years of service, he was short of just six months of luck and landed in this mess.

"I hear Eunsoo got a full-time offer from E & K. She's going to settle down in Beanstalk. Didn't she consult you?" Minso remembered someone asking him five years ago. Of course, this had been news to him. He had lost touch with Eunsoo three months earlier. They had gotten into a seemingly small fight but had not talked since. As he expected, Eunsoo had withered away in the end. She had eroded into sand, which now blew over him in the dry wind.

The hot, sandy wind jolted him awake. Judging by his blackouts, he must have lost more blood than he thought. As he felt no pain, he guessed he had hurt his neck or spine.

He would be in trouble if the enemy found him first, but in even deeper trouble if he was not found at all. He had a feeling it would come to that.

"It's a long story."

Eunsoo listened quietly to Byungsoo talk. He went on, "I don't know Mr. Kim Minso personally. The first time I heard his name was four years ago. Back then I was …"

Four years ago, Byungsoo was a public relations officer on the city's steering committee and an ordinary thirty-five-year-old office worker. Born and raised in Beanstalk, he genuinely loved his city. He found it deeply irritating whenever Beanstalk was compared to the Tower of Babel. Admittedly, Beanstalk was something of a symbol of modern capitalism, where every inch and moment on its territory was commercialized, but it was not a nest of evil to Byungsoo.

He told himself, "People who've never lived here have no clue what Beanstalk is really like."

Everyone in the neighboring country considered Beanstalk cancerous. Although the country's capital and Beanstalk had a border between them, they practically formed one society as they were almost identical in terms of language and racial makeup. Except, in that country's opinion, inhumanity and unbridled commercialism were all concentrated in Beanstalk.

Byungsoo disagreed. A completely urbanized nation did not mean life there was dry or lacking in humanity. In a society of high anonymity there formed a kind of trust that only existed between anonymous people, and in that sense Beanstalk was a city-state with impressive levels of trust in others. Locals usually pointed to the blue mailboxes beside the elevator stops as evidence.

So did Byungsoo. As one of the city's public relations officers, he went on frequent business trips across the border to persuade people that Beanstalk was not a cancer. He would often bring up the blue mailboxes on these occasions:

"Mail delivery is free in Beanstalk. You might say that makes no sense when we charge people for going just one stop on our elevators. But oddly enough, sending mail is the one thing you can do for free in Beanstalk. Of course, there's an official postal system run by the city, but we don't use it unless we're mailing important documents. That's a paid service, you see. For normal letters, we just need to address the envelope nice and clear, go to the nearest elevator stop, and pop it in the mailbox. A blue mailbox looks like a bookcase and has—well, every neighborhood is different, but—it has fifty slots, give or take. Each slot is labeled by floor number, say from floor A to B. We put our mail in the relevant slot, and voilà! The letters deliver themselves."

"Is this supposed to be a ghost story?"

"No, I meant that elevator passengers deliver the mail. Before they get on the elevator, Beanstalkians check the blue mailbox and take any mail going to the floor they're headed to. When they arrive, they drop it off at the mailbox next to the elevator. Then, the people who live on that floor come to see if they've received anything and sort the other mail into more detailed addresses. Whoever's heading there keeps on delivering. Not everyone does it, but some people obviously do because the letters get delivered."

"Wouldn't there be a lot of lost post though?"

"Not a lot, actually. Beanstalk Tacit Power Research did a study of it. While there is some difference among districts, apparently an average of 93.57 percent of mail gets delivered within two days. Even letters from across the border reach their destination 94.74 percent of the time."

"But I don't know if you can trust super important deliveries with that."

"Ah, the important letters should be sent through the paid postal service. Which doesn't mean blue mailboxes are meaningless, they're just not mainly used for work purposes."

"Then what are they for?"

"To talk. To ask after one another, share news, express feelings. Not to talk about money or lawsuits, but about people and their lives. Tens of thousands of these letters go around Beanstalk every day. That's why Beanstalk is not a Tower of Babel. Because our language never split in two."

"Even so, how can you have private conversations over a channel like that?"

"We trust each other. Absolute faith, only possible in a country with an urbanization level of one hundred percent. In Beanstalk, we trust individuals."

At moments like this, Byungsoo's audience would be struck silent. His chest would swell with pride.

Then one evening, after dragging his tired body home to Level 599, Byungsoo was trying to find receipts for meeting expenses from his last business trip across the border. As he rummaged through a briefcase he used on work trips, his eyes fell on a strange bundle of paper.

What's this?

Letters. They were from the blue mailbox. He must have forgotten that he put them in his briefcase and brought them home.

His heart sank. This was a misdelivery. When was his last business trip? He did a mental count and realized it was over four months ago. Although Byungsoo doubted the bundle contained any important letters, something gnawed at the back of his mind. He pored over the letters. He came across a postcard addressed to a Cho Eunsoo at the E & K Design Department, sent by a man named Kim Minso from the neighboring country.

I'm sorry. I want to apologize. These past ten days I've thought hard about what you said, and I admit I was too impatient. OK. Let's start over, like you said. I love you.

Oh no. Byungsoo's face flushed.

Why on earth did this guy send such an important message through a blue mailbox! Why not tell her in person? He could have told her over the phone at least.

This is not my fault, Byungsoo thought.

But it obviously was. To be fair, it was the sender's fault too. At every mailbox location, signs were invariably put up outlining instructions and disclaimers. One of the finer points included: "On average, six percent of mail or more may get lost, in which case the sender shall assume sole legal responsibility. Important records, original documents that cannot be reproduced, or letters containing personal information must be sent via the paid postal service."

I mean, when the misdelivery rate is as high as six percent, what was this dolt thinking, letting strangers deliver such an important message?

Byungsoo put the postcard back in his briefcase and went into the living room. He sat on the couch and lapsed into thought. He tried to tell himself this was no big deal. Wanting to clear his head, he switched on the TV. The award ceremony of some film festival was on, and a dog that had just won an honorary award hopped onto the stage.

"Are you going to make an acceptance speech?" The host's quip drew a roar of laughter from the audience. Byungsoo absently watched the scene. His eyes were staring intently at the TV, but his ears took in no sound. He returned to his bedroom and fished the postcard out of his briefcase again.

To: Ms. Cho Eunsoo
Design Department, E & K
Level 599

Byungsoo jumped to his feet and hurried out. He headed for the east district, where the E & K office was located. The postcard was long overdue, but better late than never.

Hang on, what should I say when I see her? Should I just stick the postcard in the mailbox and run for it? But that could complicate matters. Their situation might've changed by now.

Five minutes after setting off, Byungsoo began to have second thoughts. The situation might be resolved already as four months had passed. There were plenty of channels to communicate other than the blue mailbox. If Kim Minso didn't receive a reply after sending a message like that, he would have surely tried to contact her some other way. Unless he was stupid, he would have gotten hold of her in any way he could. Minso was bound to have contacted her, assuming he was not a fool.

Byungsoo turned back home. It was only when he reached his unit that something occurred to him: *What if he was a fool?* Shortly after returning home, Byungsoo drifted off to sleep. He woke up the next morning and went to work. He passed the day serenely until it was almost time to leave the office and the postcard crossed his mind.

Grabbing his bags as soon as the clock struck six, Byungsoo dashed to the elevator and scoured the blue mailbox. The incoming mail section was packed with letters. He set about sorting each letter by address, causing passersby to give him a warm, appreciative smile. They were probably tourists. Byungsoo did not smile back. There were no letters from Kim Minso. He did spot a few packages from across the border, so the letters in the international mailbox must have been collected.

Byungsoo went back the next day. The moment he got off work, he rushed to the mailbox on Level 599. He wanted to check it before anyone else did. Fortunately, no one seemed to have gone through it yet, so as he had the day before, he sorted the incoming mail and stacked it into different slots according to delivery address. But again, not a single letter was going to Cho Eunsoo.

Byungsoo told himself this was no cause for alarm. A lack of correspondence did not necessarily mean the couple had split up. Cho Eunsoo could have changed jobs, gone on a business trip, or a letter could have been delivered that very morning. Plus, Byungsoo couldn't jump to conclusions about their relationship status simply because they had gone two days without writing.

A week went by, then a fortnight, but still no letters from Kim Minso.

"Ms. Yang Hyunmi, you know the blue mailboxes?" asked

Byungsoo. "How do young people use them? Not everyone uses it to send letters and things to someone they're dating, right?"

"Actually, everyone does," his colleague Hyunmi replied.

"Why? Why not email or call?"

"You're asking me, sir? *You're* the city PR Officer. If we don't use it, we'd become social outcasts. What else would we use it for other than dating?"

"No, I meant couldn't there be exceptions? Maybe one in ten people."

"More like one in thirty."

"You think so?"

Byungsoo's fears appeared to be confirmed. The situation might even be worse than he had expected.

That night, Byungsoo went to see Lee Gyung-hwan, a private detective he had once hired to spy on his wife.

"What a pleasant surprise, sir. Is it your wife again?" asked Lee.

"No, not her. It's these two."

Byungsoo held out the postcard from Kim Minso. The detective examined it in silence. Then with a sly smirk, Lee said, "This must be very trying for you, sir. First your wife and now your lady friend …"

"My lady friend? What are you talking about?" said Byungsoo.

Another two weeks passed. Having paid the detective an advance with every last penny of his slush fund, Byungsoo was seized by misgivings. It was normal for couples to separate. Young people these days especially—they hooked up just so they could break up. Of course, he could not say for certain that true love was quite extinct. It was a matter of probability—the odds of Minso and Eunsoo being a pair of star-crossed lovers who had found true love was perhaps one in thirty at best.

The thought made Byungsoo want to kick himself. What was the point of spending all this money? In truth, the amount of money was not a big problem. The problem was that the money from his slush fund had all been laundered.

It would take me at least five years to build up that kind of capital again. Do I really need to go to all this trouble? Even if I clear up the misunderstanding, they probably won't live happily ever after anyway.

Byungsoo considered his own married life. It had been lousy. But whenever he remembered his delivery blunder, his face still burned with embarrassment. There was nothing else for it; he would have to straighten this mess out whether the couple stayed together or not.

Yet another week passed. When he revisited Lee Gyung-hwan's office, the detective chuckled unpleasantly, "Your lady friend sure was an eyeful."

Byungsoo headed back home with the detective's report.

Although the public nature of his job required that he have a happy family, in reality his wife was never home unless required. Then, in times of need, she would come back and play the part of the good wife and mother. She did not do a slap-dash job of it either. In fact, her performance was impeccable. Byungsoo was at once impressed and unnerved on more than one occasion. "What is it you want?" he had often asked her, but his wife would not reply. She would simply leave the apartment without a word.

She was away that day too. Byungsoo walked into a home that did not exude an ounce of warmth. As Byungsoo recalled memories of his marriage, he opened the envelope from Lee. On top of the enclosed papers he saw a photograph of Eunsoo, who looked exhausted and burnt-out. Another photo showed Minso looking as if he had given up on life.

I found nothing on them. There has been zero contact.

That was the conclusion Lee Gyung-hwan had drawn. But Byungsoo was even more troubled by Minso's recent activity.

Kim Minso recently applied for a contractor job in the Beanstalk Navy. His application was for an additional four-year enlistment and overseas tour. Since he finished service in his own country, he will likely be awarded extra immigration points. As you may be aware, applicants for Beanstalkian citizenship can earn twenty-seven percent extra points by completing four years of overseas service. This appears to be what Kim Minso is after.

This was utter stupidity. The Navy? When he had already served his full military term? Minso seemed bent on getting into Beanstalk at whatever cost. What foolishness. Could his heart stay foolish after four years? Would Eunsoo even be in Beanstalk then? Surely not. Surely, things would change. Minso could not go on being twenty-five when he turned twenty-nine. The twenty-five in him would wither into nothing before the four years were up, and only then would Beanstalk grant him citizenship. Wasn't this arrogance what gave Beanstalk the nickname "Babel"?

Putting the papers down, Byungsoo went into his wife's

room. Thick dust covered where there should have been signs of life. The residue from his wife weathering away. He sat alone in his wife's empty room for a long time, pondering. If he and his wife had somehow managed to communicate each other's feelings and avoid misunderstanding, would this room still be empty?

Argh, what am I getting myself into for this fool?

Byungsoo called up his old classmate who was working in the Navy and offered a few words of "advice" on hiring contractors.

His old classmate said, "Kim Minso? Sure, hiring him isn't a problem, but what's up? You're not one to ask these kinds of favors. He a friend of yours?"

"Not in the least. Just do me this favor, alright?"

That was all Byungsoo could do to help.

But had he made the right choice? The question kept plaguing him. But this was already four years ago.

I shouldn't have helped him get the pilot position. Flying is supposed to be much safer than sailing. That poor bastard has the worst luck.

Byungsoo's reverie was interrupted by Eunsoo: "Where in the Taklamakan is he lost?"

"They're trying to find his exact location," Byungsoo replied.

"So, you don't know yet. If he's been shot down, does that mean he might already be dead?"

Byungsoo nodded quietly. He added, "But there's a good chance he's alive. The faster the rescue team gets there, the higher his chances of survival. Trouble is, it doesn't look like rescue operations will start any time soon."

"Why not? A jet's been downed."

"The Beanstalk Defense Forces aren't supposed to be there. If they act now, they would essentially be admitting to a preemptive strike attempt on that missile base."

"But how can they not do anything when one of their own men crashed in the middle of the desert?"

"Well, technically speaking, Mr. Kim Minso isn't considered a Beanstalkian airman. He's an employee of a defense contractor hired by the Beanstalk Navy, not a pilot belonging to the Navy itself …"

Eunsoo opened her mouth to say something but stopped and fiddled with her teacup.

"So what can I do for you?" she asked finally.

"I wanted to give you this."

Byungsoo held out the postcard Minso had written four years ago to Eunsoo. "This is the postcard I told you about. It's very late, but I wanted to give this to you now rather than later, which is why I'm here."

However, he could not bring himself to mention that he was the one who helped Minso become a Navy aviator. He had come to tell her as much, but he sensed that she did not want to hear that sort of information.

Eunsoo peered at the postcard. The handwriting was unmistakably Minso's. An old memory rushed back to her.

"Eunsoo, I'm scared you're going to waste away," Minso had said.

"Oh, please not that again. Why do you keep going on

about that? Tell me, did I ever say I wanted to break up?"

"It's just, I feel like that's what's going to happen if you go there."

Eunsoo had been irritated by those words back then. By Minso's expression when he said them, by his theatrical, dejected voice. Why had his apologies not felt like apologies? At the time, everything he said had seemed like lies.

"Cut it out, Kim Minso! You're acting heartbroken to guilt trip me."

Eunsoo remembered saying that to Minso. What had she been thinking? What exactly had she wanted to hear? Even now, Minso was trapped inside the postcard, apologizing endlessly.

"Please don't beat yourself up," Eunsoo told Byungsoo. "Even if this postcard had been delivered on time, I'm sure Minso and I'd have gotten into another fight. We had so many reasons to fight. We didn't break up because I didn't receive this postcard. I've always thought we slowly drifted apart; I didn't even realize there might've been another reason until you mentioned it. Besides, I'm engaged to someone now, and I'm not so unhappy as to desperately wish things had worked out with Minso."

She meant it. Eunsoo was a full-time satellite designer at E & K now. She had gotten her dream job, and she had met great people. Beanstalk had not disappointed her. One undelivered postcard did not change that.

"As for Minso's current situation, I'm sorry I can't be of any help," Eunsoo added.

"No problem," replied Byungsoo.

Byungsoo exchanged courtesies with Eunsoo and stood up to leave, feeling dispirited. He regretted meeting her.

What did I come here to do? I came to communicate something to her, but what? I'm sure I didn't come just to give her this postcard. I wanted to communicate something before the body's found.

Byungsoo returned to his office. Minso's crash point was still unknown. It was because the jet he had flown out on was not equipped with the Navy's tracking device. Even if a full-scale search party was sent out immediately, there was a slim chance of finding the pilot before it was too late.

The Navy intended to abandon Minso. It had as good as given up on him already. The Defense Forces had no intention of deploying any official units to search for him. Instead, they secured civilian rescue helicopters that did not bear Beanstalk military insignia from areas near the desert. They had only rounded up six such helicopters, which was nowhere near enough to search the entire Taklamakan Desert in the next day or two.

The situation was in the enemy's favor. According to intelligence reports, Cosmomafia had already claimed all the routes leading into the area where Minso was downed. With historic links to the former Soviet Union, the militant group had the missile technology to intercept satellites. It had recently expanded its list of targets to include not only military satellites but also civilian ones, emerging as the largest threat to Beanstalk's biggest industry, global satellite services. The Beanstalk Defense Forces' official stance towards Cosmomafia was to always strike first. However, they could not simply send bombers to hit Cosmomafian anti-satellite bases in a country that does not condone pre-emptive strikes. In cases like this, the Navy hired personnel through civilian defense contractors. It recruited mercenary pilots as leased employees who would work for, but never belong to, the Beanstalk military and used them to execute bombings. This meant the Navy would hold zero responsibility for any problems that might arise. In short, the Navy had never planned on saving Minso. It was casting him aside, following a policy it created seven years ago.

"We can't take risks when we don't know if he's still alive or not."

"Shouldn't that be, we can't give up yet precisely because we don't know if he's still alive or not?"

"Well, it's not like he's our citizen."

The Beanstalkian constitution did not limit the Defense Forces' responsibilities to protecting only the lives and property of its citizens, because Beanstalk was originally just a building instead of a nation. Initially, the Defense Forces' duty was not to categorize people into nationalities but to ensure the safety of both residents and visitors. That was the true Beanstalk way. Beanstalk's humility meant that it was not simply another Babel. But that was no longer the Beanstalk way, it seemed. The Beanstalk Byungsoo knew was mere promotional rhetoric now.

There was no way to turn Beanstalk back to what it had been. Resourceful civil servant though he was, Byungsoo was incapable of conjuring up on a moment's notice the enormous amount of equipment needed to rescue a pilot downed in foreign territory. The most he had managed to do was to rent two firefighting helicopters for two days.

If only I could try finding him by satellite.

But the Navy would never release a military satellite image. Its official position on the incident was: "We are not aware of any such occurrence." Even if Byungsoo obtained the image, poring over a photograph of the entire Taklamakan Desert unaided by professional analysts was a reckless undertaking that was not worth attempting.

I should get the military to act.

Byungsoo rang up an aide to a councilor on the National Defense Committee, reached out to his newspaper contacts, and explained the situation to activists at private organizations whom he had met several times, but their responses were the same: there was little they could do. The situation was impossible to resolve unless the government stepped in.

The councilor's aide, who was Byungsoo's old college friend, said, "You know during World War I, the German fleet never even got as far as the North Sea. But if you look at the British Navy's internal documents, there was serious talk of losing the war against Germany. Why? Although the mainland wasn't under attack, British trade routes were almost cut off because of Germany's unrestricted submarine warfare. It was 'unrestricted' but really, there were only thirty-odd German U-boats out in the Atlantic. Same with Beanstalk. Are ships more expensive, or are satellites? Even if Beanstalk Tower is safe, a blow to its satellites will jeopardize the country. So, Beanstalk isn't going to change its position, and it'll never send out a rescue team."

Byungsoo clenched his fists.

Elsewhere, Eunsoo also sat clenching her fists, glaring at the tabletop.

"Cho Eunsoo, aren't you going to eat? Is the salad talking to you?"

"What? Oh, sorry. I was thinking about something."

"So it's today, huh? The day that supposedly comes around once a quarter—Cho Eunsoo's Thinking Day."

"Ha ha, very funny."

Eunsoo's mind wandered again. Her fiancé, Jinsoo, didn't push the conversation either. *How was Minso now? Was he alive? As he'd fallen in the middle of the desert, perhaps being alive was the more painful outcome. Why did he enlist when he didn't even enjoy being in the military during his service? He had come close to deserting when he was a conscript. And when did he learn to fly? To think that he'd trained only to get himself into this wreck. Strange. It wasn't like Minso at all to behave this way. Why? Was it really because of that postcard?* If so, it would be her fault. *No, it couldn't be, he wasn't stupid. Wait.* She remembered he was.

"Jinsoo."

"Yes?"

"Can you rent me a satellite?"

"A satellite?"

"Why? For how long?"

"I don't know, maybe twenty seconds?"

"What do you need it for?"

"I want to take a photograph. Of the entire Taklamakan Desert. It has to be high resolution."

"Yeah? I'll look into it tomorrow."

TOWER

"I need it now."

"Now?"

"The sooner the better ..."

"Right this minute? Twenty seconds, huh. Is this for personal use? I'm guessing it's not for work."

"No, it's not. Is it expensive?"

"I guess there're both expensive and cheap options. Let me check the timetable. Would the resolution for tourist site images be enough? You wouldn't be able to see faces close-up though. But it'd be affordable. And any satellite passing over there shouldn't be booked at this hour."

"OK. Can you rent it with your employee discount?"

"Jeez, I save a damsel in distress only to have her rob me? I can see you're up to something alright. Taklamakan, huh. What is it this time? Are you stalking an ex that got away or something?"

When Eunsoo nodded, Jinsoo snickered.

Eunsoo phoned Byungsoo. She told him about the satellite image. Byungsoo listened quietly for a while, before interrupting, "I can get satellite photos on my end too. But we need a much higher-res image to run it through a computer. Even if the jet were in one piece, making out its shape might be next to impossible depending on how it's positioned on the ground. As we don't have much to go on except smashed bits and pieces, imagine how much harder that would be. Even more so with a blurry image."

"Can't computers still read the image? Is there no other way? What if we were to go over it manually?"

"We could do that, except we'd need a hundred people

checking the image for five years to find him. Those aren't exact numbers, but you get my point. We'd find him eventually, but who's to know when?"

"Let's get a higher res image, then."

"I've been trying to, but they wouldn't give it to me. The Navy, I mean."

After ending the call, Eunsoo asked Jinsoo if Byungsoo's information was accurate.

"Of course, he's right. Even if you can get a sharper image, it'd be useless without the software to analyze it. The military owns that technology, so you can't use that either. You're really cooking up some scheme, aren't you?"

"Yes." Eunsoo's shoulders slumped. "Because of some dummy."

"I see, this is for a dummy. Something tells me I'm not supposed to ask who this dummy is. Anyway, you don't need me to rent the tourism satellite anymore, right?"

Eunsoo replied, "Actually, I do."

"Why?"

"Just because."

"Dummy."

It was early evening. Eunsoo came back home and switched on her computer. Then, with a satellite image viewer, she pulled up a satellite picture of the Taklamakan Desert. She zoomed in on a section and examined the image in greater detail. She needed more detail, just a little more. She zoomed in as far as she could. The portion of the image she saw onscreen grew smaller and smaller. Nothing was there. The Taklamakan was a sand desert. Ancient oasis cities or winding silk roads might lie somewhere in its midst, but Eunsoo could not know where just by scanning the picture. All she saw were sand dunes.

Eunsoo zoomed out until the whole image was visible on the screen. This was a picture of Minso. She had no idea where he was, but she knew he was definitely in there.

What are you doing out there, dummy.

The phone blared. Eunsoo was filled with foreboding.

"Hey, it's me." It was her friend. A sense of anticlimax washed over Eunsoo. "Is everything OK? Why do you sound so startled? Were you doing something naughty?"

"Nothing naughty per se, but I was looking at a picture of my ex," replied Eunsoo.

"Oho, enjoying your last days of being single, I see."

"Yeah, I don't know what I'm doing."

"Is he cute? Send me the pic online. I want to see."

"You do? I wonder if you'd be able to see him though."

Eunsoo put down the phone. She was gripped by sudden apprehension and called Byungsoo again.

"I'll look for him myself," declared Eunsoo. "Even if the Navy doesn't know exactly where he crashed, wouldn't they have a rough idea of where he might be? Can you try to find out?"

Byungsoo replied, "As I said, this isn't something you can do alone. Rescue helicopters have gone out to search, so let's wait and see."

"I just feel so restless not doing anything. Can you tell me which way the rescue helicopters were generally headed? Then we'll know where the Navy suspects he is."

"I wouldn't bank on the Navy knowing anything. They seem pretty clueless too."

"Then I'll look where the helicopters haven't looked yet. You said there isn't anything else we can do anyway. I'd be able to do at least one helicopter's share of work, wouldn't I? I've got to try. Even if I can't find him."

One helicopter's share of work.

"OK. Give me a minute."

Byungsoo hung up and called a private environmental monitoring agency, based across the border, that received funding support from the Beanstalk Public Relations Bureau.

"It's not an order," said Byungsoo. "I'm asking a favor. I just need you to set up a website. I've got a situation here. Yes, we have servers here too, but—sticky situation, you know. We can't set it up ourselves—our government can't be involved. You can take it down after, say, two days. That's right. Uh-huh. That's right. Of course not. Why would I ask you if this puts you at risk? Come on, you know me. Yes. And I'll send you a satellite image, so if you can put that up on the site. Oh, and one more thing …"

Byungsoo got the satellite image from Eunsoo. He tried to find one with a higher resolution, but there were no suitable satellites passing over the desert. As soon as he received the image, he ran to IT and asked them to draw gridlines over it.

For an untrained eye to spot the crash point based on plane debris alone, the grid had to be divided into fairly small squares so that when you zoomed in on one, you could see the image in sufficient detail.

"How many squares do we have?" asked Byungsoo.

"About two hundred thousand," his colleague in the IT department replied.

Supposing one person took thirty minutes to search a square, it would take a hundred people a thousand hours to search the full image.

If I get ten people or so from the Public Relations Bureau to help, and factor in the number of helicopters …

It would still take around a year. Six months if they narrowed down the search by half to priority areas. This was a lost cause. But he could not sit and do nothing, not when he had just heard someone say she would take on one helicopter's share of work. He forwarded the gridded image to the environmental monitoring agency and dialed Eunsoo.

"Ms. Cho Eunsoo, can you stop what you're doing and take care of something for me? I had the image uploaded to another server. I'll give you the link—you'll be able to access it in an hour. But before that, I need you to do something. Since I can't get the administration to act …"

While the government sat idle, individuals dashed around Beanstalk. Eunsoo wrote to her acquaintances.

My dearest colleague Gyunghee,

I moved into Beanstalk four years ago. I've fulfilled my dreams here and I couldn't be happier. Yet, when I moved here, I left someone behind across the border. He was a smart, kind person. All these years I've been too busy to think about him, but I finally received news today.

At this very moment, he is stranded in the desert, a downed mercenary pilot of the Beanstalk Navy. He extended his military service for an overseas tour in hopes of obtaining citizenship. I want to believe that he didn't do this for me, but knowing he can be a fool, I can't be sure. He was shot down in the Taklamakan Desert, but the Navy is doing nothing to save him, claiming it has no jurisdiction over the matter, turning a deaf ear.

Dear Gyunghee, and beloved citizens of Beanstalk, your government has given up on him. For he is not a Beanstalkian citizen. But it is my belief that you will not do the same. A rectangular border may be drawn across the twenty-second floor of Beanstalk, but I know your hearts are not confined to a box.

I've secured a satellite image and am looking for his crashed jet. While he lies abandoned in the desert alone, I wander that desert on my own to find him. He could be seriously injured or dead. After tonight, the latter will become more likely. Desert winds may also blow sand over the aircraft debris.

Please help me by going to this link. There, you will find the image divided into squares. The squares I have already checked are marked blue. Those I am checking are green. Click on an unmarked square and look for any signs of the jet. The more squares you check the better, but if you can, please check at least two, or even just one.

Eunsoo couldn't write a new letter for every intended recipient. But she put her heart into every word. She printed multiple copies of the letter, handwrote the names of recipients one by one along with their addresses, and put them in the blue mailbox. Some of them were addressed to people at the Public Relations Bureau. Then, she went back home and opened the satellite file.

Byungsoo told his entire team to leave work early.

"But we're on standby in case of a PR emergency."

"Just go. Listen, go to the blue mailbox next to the elevator on Level 599, and deliver everything that's in it. Some of the letters should be addressed to you. Read your letter and do whatever it tells you to do. Make ten copies and send them to your friends. Consider it overtime, and keep at it until two a.m.—no, four a.m.—and don't worry about coming to the office in the morning. Got it?"

Returning to his seat, Byungsoo pulled up the satellite image. Three squares had already turned blue. Their goal was to get a hundred and fifty people to help, including Eunsoo's acquaintances as well as friends and family of his staff. It was pyramid scheme-style recruitment, but they had no other choice. They would try it—they had nothing to lose.

Byungsoo clicked on a square and enlarged it. He saw no sand dunes and even spotted some green here and there, but the landscape still seemed dry and hopelessly vast. There was nothing. Although he was not peering into the universe, only a tiny fragment of the Earth's surface, nature was so boundlessly immense that most of the things in that fragment looked utterly insignificant. Even so, he could leave no stone unturned, nor presume there was nothing. Had he checked thoroughly? He kept doubting his own eyes. Had he perhaps zoned out for a split second and missed a spot? He scanned and rescanned the same places before finishing the square. This took him forty minutes, but the search was fruitless. Byungsoo marked the square as completed on the map.

When he zoomed out to the full image, he saw that seven

squares were checked and five were being checked. Five other people were working online.

He turned back to the desert.

The blue mailboxes were modeled after an internal document delivery network used by SATlease, a satellite leasing service. When it was founded, SATlease occupied a tall, narrow space in the south district of Beanstalk from Level 394 to 472, which made it time-consuming to send documents up and down the floors. In an attempt to save costs, the company set up a test document station that was just like the current blue mailboxes. The experiment failed. The daily delivery rate stopped at only ninety percent. On the other hand, office romances grew fivefold. SATlease shut down its document delivery network, but Beanstalk created the blue mailbox. Not for efficiency, but for human connection.

Eunsoo's letters began to circulate. They left Level 599 and traveled quickly down to Level 450 and up to Level 600. The Public Relations Bureau staff were hand-delivering them to blue mailboxes. Within thirty minutes of having delivered them all, the bureau staff made even more copies of Eunsoo's letter and fired them off across the building. There were now slightly over three hundred letters, which were not travelling very quickly due to the late hour. But thanks to Beanstalk's large population of night owls—something that always astonished foreign tourists—the speed of delivery never quite slowed to zero.

Two hours later, new letters were sent out. Not by Eunsoo, nor any of the bureau staff. They were mailed from places that Byungsoo could never have guessed. The same thing was happening in other parts of Beanstalk: letters were generating more letters, which were generating even more.

Having been lost inside the desert for hours, Eunsoo finally zoomed out to the satellite orbit screen for a quick break. She lifted her gaze slightly, and only then did she register the real world outside her monitor.

Her eyes hurt. Maybe she was imagining it, but her eyes felt dry after staring at the desert for so long. She put a few eyedrops in her desert eyes and returned to her map. A strange sight met her eyes. She called Byungsoo.

"I think something's wrong with the website," Eunsoo said.

Byungsoo exited the desert view and looked at the full map. The entire northeast section was blue.

"You're right," agreed Byungsoo. "What time is it? I'm not sure if they'll pick up this late, but I'll try to find out what's going on and get back to you."

Byungsoo phoned the environmental monitoring agency that had created the website. His call was picked up immediately.

Surprised, Byungsoo asked, "What are you doing up this late?"

"Huh?" said his contact at the agency. "I'm working on the thing—that thing you gave me earlier."

"What? Setting up the website? But you've already done that."

"Yeah, but I'm searching too. On my fifth square now."

"You are? Why?"

"To look for that person."

"Person? How'd you know about that?"

"What do you mean how? The whole country's buzzing about it! Everyone's been busting their butts all night, and the man who started it doesn't know?"

"What are you talking about?"

"I'm saying there's 27,470 users right now."

"Users?"

"Users on the site I made for you, of course. They're searching for the jet that crashed in the Taklamakan Desert."

Byungsoo was suddenly wide awake. "How can twenty-seven thousand people be online this late? It's the middle of the night."

"Oh, let's see. There's a little over six thousand from Beanstalk, another five thousand from my country, and the rest are from other countries."

"But why?"

"What do you mean 'why'? They're just searching, that's all."

"I know, but why them? Are you sure this isn't a bug or something?"

"There's no bug. What's there to be a bug, it's just a simple picture file. The letter Ms. Cho Eunsoo sent around Beanstalk was translated and forwarded to other countries. So, they're searching, just because. Do they need a reason? You know how these things work on the Internet. People just do it."

In an hour, the user count hit over forty thousand. An hour later, seventy-five thousand. More and more blue squares lit up. A green band was rapidly forming around the blue squares like a ring of fire. Byungsoo stopped searching and gaped at his screen. He could not make sense of what he saw.

Neither could Eunsoo. She was stunned when she heard it wasn't a bug.

"If it's not a bug, what is it?" she had asked.

"You tell me," Byungsoo replied.

By daybreak, no less than 220,000 people were double-checking the squares that had been marked blue. As Minso was still missing even after the whole map had turned blue, someone must have overlooked him.

Soon, a new website appeared. Byungsoo told Eunsoo about it over the phone. Created in Germany, the site not only showed whether the squares had been checked, but also made them a darker shade of blue every time they were rechecked.

Then, 340,000 people set to work again. Within half an hour, that number soared to 500,000. In the blink of an eye, the map turned several shades darker, creating the illusion that the contour lines of the desert were shooting up in altitude.

Eunsoo gazed at the map. Progressively turning a deeper blue, the Taklamakan Desert looked as if it were slowly being lifted to the sky. As if people were offering up the desert and the missing contract pilot to the heavens through sheer will.

Five minutes past seven a.m. Beanstalk time, a red dot popped up on the map. Eunsoo's phone rang. It was Byungsoo.

"We found him."

In that instant, the number of users flickered before Eunsoo's eyes.

2,774,867.

When she magnified the blinking red dot, she saw an unconscious Minso. Tears stung her eyes.

Byungsoo said, "He's managed to get out of the aircraft, but he seems badly injured."

"When will the rescue squad …?" Eunsoo couldn't finish her sentence.

"I've told them his location. They should be flying out now."

Minso jerked awake. He had the feeling he was being watched. But there was no one in the vicinity. As he slipped in and out of consciousness, he mused that the threshold for death was too high.

I must still be alive. Is it always this hard to die?

The world was awfully quiet. Even if he hadn't crashed in the middle of the desert, at that moment when his body had cut itself off from the outside world, any place he was stranded in would be no different from a desert.

Maybe he had always been living in such a deserted state. Even when his limbs were sound and his nerves in working order, the world might have been a meaningless place all along. Things like love, grief, and regret might have been mere mirages created by his senses.

What am I thinking? Is this enlightenment?

Strangely enough, all of a sudden he wished to enter nirvana. Despite believing in one God for two decades, when faced with a life-and-death situation, Buddhist enlightenment seemed easier to achieve than Christian salvation.

I can't believe I'm having these crazy thoughts. Maybe it's not my time to die just yet.

Minso lost consciousness.

He came around moments later. Once more, he felt someone staring down at him from above. The sensation was so strong that he knew his time had finally come.

This must be God. The gaze filled his entire soul. The gates to heaven had opened. Somewhere in the distance, Minso heard the Angel of the Lord flying toward him. The loud flapping of God's messenger rather sounded like the engine of an HH-60G.

This is bizarre. This isn't how it should go.

God's helicopter hovered above his head. Minso was stumped. His story had swapped genres. Now he was too intrigued to enter nirvana.

The Elevator Maneuver Exercise

Strictly speaking, I am not a verticalist. I'm just a government transportation official. There are people who mistake me for a verticalist because my nose is buried in an elevator map every day, but think about it: do you honestly think I can do what I do by only factoring in vertical transport?

There are people who keep drawing distinctions between verticalists and horizontalists, trying to force one label or the other on me, but I'm not even sure if they truly understand what "v-winger" and "h-winger" mean. The concepts actually originated from "Vertical Transportation Cooperative" and "Horizontal Transportation Labor Union." Lots of people assume that elevators are Beanstalk's only method of transportation since it's a skyscraper, but this place isn't just long from top to bottom; it's also pretty long when you measure it horizontally. That's why there are quite a few people in the horizontal transport industry. There always have been, including when Beanstalk was being constructed. Hoisting up construction supplies with a crane isn't the end of it; ferrying them across a floor is an equally big job. A job that at the end of the day still has to be done by hand. Moving walkways are installed in some areas, but they're not built for freight. It's a menial job, really. It requires muscle, not expertise or capital.

The Vertical Transportation Cooperative, on the other hand, has a completely different vibe. Even the cargo handlers there rarely use the term "labor union"; instead, they say "cooperative" without mentioning the word "workers." This business involves hauling things up on elevators, so the equipment is more important than human labor. Which is why this side gives off a more capitalist vibe, whereas horizontal labor unions feel more like the labor unions of old. Kids these days don't know all this history and assume verticalism is categorically a rich people's ideology and horizontalism a poor people's one. But it's not so simple. We can't solve the problems of our lives with just one approach or the other, can we? When one side sends things up on elevators, the other side has to move them to their destination to complete the delivery.

My job works exactly like that. Just look at the contingency deployment plan for the Army. We call it the Elevator Maneuver Exercise for the sake of convenience, but there's no way it can be done by elevators alone. When transferring forces from the Level 22 border to Level 670 and deploying them to precisely where they're needed in battle, horizontal marching speed is just as critical as vertical transport speed.

You need to balance the two in order to properly execute a deployment.

If you let me be fancy for a minute: isn't life like that too? How can this complicated thing we call life fit neatly into v-wing, h-wing? Take me for example. My family used to be filthy rich. You know the basketball court on Level 77? That was my father's. The ticket sales weren't stellar because the home team performed terribly, but performance wasn't important anyway—the value of the real estate kept rising.

I don't know if it's still running, but there's an old weather satellite way up somewhere in the sky. It was an old, useless piece of junk, but my father must've heard something from someone because he went right ahead and bought it. He didn't buy it alone but joined some investment fund which required him to put down the basketball court and all his assets as collateral. The loan he took out was stupendous. I wondered what on earth he'd do with that piece of junk after going to such lengths to buy it. It was probably worth less than scrap metal, but why was it so expensive? Turns out that rumors of redevelopment had made the rounds. My father didn't need the weather satellite but its orbit. It was a stationary satellite, you see. A stationary satellite orbits as fast as the Earth rotates, so from Earth it looks like it's always at the same spot. Apparently, the rumors had involved something about a space station being constructed on that orbit. Hence my father investing his whole fortune in what he thought was the opportunity of a lifetime.

But then the global financial market crashed again and wiped out all plans for redevelopment, not to mention the space station. That's when things went downhill for my family. More like down the drain. It was spectacular.

My mother made her own contribution to a family already in shambles. She scraped up our remaining fortune, down to the last coin, and ran off with some dude. I don't know how she pilfered the money. It was decades ago now, but how she did it is still beyond the likes of me. I could study it for another ten years and never get it. She fled overseas, and my father passed away two years later. My father was like that. He was such a social man that when he was declared socially dead, he died biologically too.

I was left with a single room, one of the tiny apartments people called "exam-crammer rooms" crowded together on Level 520. Mine came with its own bathroom. This unit was the only asset that my mother had left under my name as her final act of maternal duty before taking off to another country.

You think she was heartless? Well, given that one exam-crammer room in Beanstalk is worth three apartments in the neighboring country, she wasn't *that* heartless. Since I owned the place instead of renting it, I would've been perfectly well-off had I sold it and moved to the neighboring country. But I was a clueless twenty-year-old back then. Born and raised in Beanstalk, I assumed something terrible would happen if I ventured outside. I was at a loss as to how to live my life. I thought I was destitute.

What really did it for me was the unusually bitter winter that year. The exam-crammer room district on the Level 500s was especially cold in winters. Some people blame the large vent that passes nearby, but in any case, it was freezing. And with the temperature being much lower that year than the previous year, everyone in that neighborhood went through living hell.

As for me, I was warm for the first month. The heating facilities themselves weren't bad. But then the utilities bill came and bam, I swear my heart stopped when I saw it. The heating cost was just ... sheesh. I worked part-time for three months to pay it off. I was the only one actually studying for the civil service exam in that so-called exam-crammer room neighborhood, but I was too busy to read a single word for three whole months, I tell you. The exam was right around the corner, yet I couldn't remember what was what when I looked at my books. The damn unit didn't have a shred of warmth as it hadn't been heated for three months. I couldn't even sleep at night from shivering. And did I have anywhere else to go during the day? Of course not, I couldn't afford to go anywhere.

One day, I was sitting at my desk wrapped in three layers of blankets, blowing warm air on my hands as I flipped the pages of my book, when my life flashed before my eyes and I had no idea how to go on living. I couldn't afford my college tuition, let alone my cram school fees, but taking time off might result in a permanent break from my studies. Then again, I wasn't cut out for work, nor did I have any relatives to help. I'd hit a dead end. It's funny looking back on it now, but I really thought so back then. That's how despair works. You sink deeper the more you think about it because you can't see your situation objectively. I even thought of suicide. Not that I'd gone so far as to plan it, I was only starting to vaguely contemplate it. Still, those three months were tough.

Then, I came down with the flu, and forget suicide, I couldn't even lift a finger as I lay there thinking this was how I was going to go. If I was that sick, you'd think I'd switch on the heat for a bit, right? The notion that using the heater would lead to catastrophe was stuck so stubbornly in my head that the option didn't even cross my mind despite my condition. I didn't dare keep the heated floor mat on for too long either.

I was lying alone in my pitch-dark room, quietly dying, when I felt a faint warmth in the darkness. I thought maybe this was how you died in your sleep and drifted off. But I was still alive when I woke up in the morning; I'd simply had a good night's sleep. I felt much better too, after sleeping so well.

Thing is, the cold that night had been no joke. It was the last cold spell of the year, and I heard some people outside Beanstalk actually died. Here, sleeping "outdoors" never exposes you to the night winds, but down there, you literally have to sleep in the open.

You know how I survived that night? It was thanks to my neighbor. My neighbor on the other side of the wall.

Someone had just moved in, and they turned their heater on so high that the warmth seeped all the way into my room. They didn't do it for my benefit of course, but that warmth was what kept me going for another year. They saved my life.

The following winter, my neighbor was away for a week. Let me tell you, that's when it became crystal clear whom I owed my life to. I thought I was going to freeze to death the whole week. Then, on exactly the eighth day, my neighbor's wall started giving off a sweet warmth and, my god, was I glad. What I felt was almost love. The most devoted, absolute love. You can laugh. I mean, to be so unconditionally glad that someone was back when I didn't even know their face— that's love in its simplest form, don't you think?

While I saved heating costs that way, I worked odd jobs and joined a horizontal labor union. I didn't work full-time as I had to keep studying for the civil service exam. I worked for movers, delivered groceries—I did whatever paid. Having done all that, I understand why horizontalist subversives harp on about "sacred muscle." Verticalist snobs don't know what that means so they laugh and mock. But you see, the value of laboring to change your life is incomparably greater than the satisfaction of working out at the gym.

It was precisely that feeling that gave me new life. I started studying again. I couldn't devote as much time as other people did, but I studied with a lot more concentration. I was happy to get even that much studying done because I didn't despair anymore.

One day after I had settled down, I became curious about the woman next door. Yes, I knew my neighbor was a woman. I could hear her voice sometimes, though I couldn't make out the words. I never saw her face since the other side of the wall wasn't part of the exam-crammer district. You've probably felt this when you walk around Beanstalk, but there are loads of places that you have no idea how to get to even though they're right next to you. Her house was exactly like that. Our walls were joined and the occasional sound carried over, but I couldn't figure out which damn alley the house sat on no matter how long I peered at the map. It wasn't as if I could drill through the wall. I gave up wondering after a while.

I passed the exam in the end. If I hadn't, I wouldn't be sitting here. I started at the Beanstalk Security Guardhouse's Transportation Planning Division right away. I'd become a verticalist snob too.

But I must have had excellent moral fiber for a verticalist snob. About two years after I joined the Transportation Planning Division, I sold my place and moved to a decent house on Level 407, and *then* the news broke that my old exam-crammer neighborhood would be included in the city outskirts' elevator redevelopment zone. Housing prices skyrocketed. Everyone in that neighborhood was a tenant, so the price hike wouldn't do them any favors, whereas I'd been an owner. I'd completely missed out on the chance to make a huge profit.

I should've known better, working in the very government division that approved the redevelopment. I was the biggest fool if ever there was one. But my stupidity must have looked like moral fiber to my division head because I was shipped off to another division. I learned later on that the Transportation Planning Division was no place for moral fiber.

My new team was called the Mobilization Planning Division at the time, under the Office of the Army Staff. Now it's called the Strategic Planning Division. Beanstalk has reserve forces of around forty thousand and about forty assembly points throughout the whole building. My division had to draw up killer plans to move forty thousand people to the Level 22 border zone at once. Let's say we put fifteen fully armed soldiers in each elevator, then we'd have to send down nearly twenty-seven hundred elevators to the frontline.

And it's not like everybody else stops using elevators because it's wartime. The Office of the Army Staff does have control over elevators in times of war, but it can't realistically requisition all elevators since the economy has to keep rolling.

That's what I did every day in the Mobilization Planning Division—I made elevator timetables. Just like the German General Staff had wrestled with creating railway timetables during World War I. But scheduling trains isn't too hard since you only need to think in two dimensions. We had to work with a three-dimensional space. And let me tell you, making only one mobilization plan doesn't cut it. Think about it. Wars don't always play out the same way. And the resources available for mobilization also change every year. We drafted twenty-three mobilization plans at the time.

As if that wasn't enough, the higher-ups created what they called the "Nonplan Room." It was an ER of sorts. When something happened that even twenty-three mobilization plans couldn't predict, the Nonplan Room was responsible for cranking out a new mobilization plan from scratch in several hours. It was a chamber of horrors.

And guess what, I was transferred there. I must've come off as having moral fiber. That was already my third year as a civil servant, by which time I'd learned the craft of taking bribes and had actually received some, but the higher-ups must have thought I still had a long way to go in that regard.

I didn't have a choice. They told me to move, so I did. But

boy, I thought that place would finish me. Twice a year we did what's called a maneuver exercise, which is basically like having to pass the civil service exam every six months. The Chief of Staff of the Army personally came up with the questions, springing simulated war conditions on us. The questions were weird too.

"An enemy aircraft on a suicide bombing mission has crashed into Beanstalk Tower at district X on the east side of Level 327. The building's outer wall is damaged and five thousand lightly armed enemy soldiers have infiltrated through the gap …"

Now that makes no sense. How can five thousand enemy soldiers crawl through a hole in Level 327? Anyway, when the Chief of Staff threw a situation at us, the generals decided on a response. The rest was pure logistical nightmare for us. All the generals had to do was *say* the response, for example, "Quickly deploy the mobile strike force, move the injured to safety, and mobilize two thousand reservists from military district Y …" but we couldn't just do that, could we? Imagine trying to draw up a transportation plan for two thousand soldiers in seventeen minutes, sheesh.

We prepared three months for each exercise. What was worse, a maneuver exercise didn't end with simply writing a plan, we had to prove that plan worked by testing it out on a small group of around two hundred soldiers. So our job was clearly more demanding than the civil service exam because we had to take this practical exam right after. In fact, some people jumped ship, took the National Bar Exam, and became judges. As for me, well, it was too late to go down that route.

Every year was tough, but the maneuver exercise in my third year at the Nonplan Room was probably the worst. While our teamwork was improving, we hadn't perfected it yet. The day we did though, even the higher-ups began to see us in a new light. Anyway, things were still rough before then.

The situation we were given for that year's maneuver exercise was especially off-kilter. It couldn't be any more bizarre: the Office of the Army Staff had staged a coup and half of Beanstalk's active forces were already in the Chief of Staff's hands. Meaning there were fewer deployable soldiers, not to mention the fact that the generals under the Office of the Army Staff couldn't be called on for help. The majority of the Office of the Army Staff was supposed to be in on the coup. In short, the mobilization system was bonkers.

But what could we do? We had to try our best. The field commander, who was a de facto general and later served as a minister, gave the order for total mobilization in military districts with available reservists and for the security guards to buy time while troops advanced toward the insurgents. It sounded like a pretty good plan: drive the insurgents into a five hundred-meter radius on Level 450 and surround them from eight directions concurrently. The bulk of the counter-insurgent forces would drive them up from below as the reservists cut off their retreat to play for time.

Problem was, the assembly point for mobilized reservists had to be dead on for that plan to work. It couldn't be too close to the insurgents nor too far from the battlefield, as the reservists had to surround the enemy three-dimensionally the moment they finished assembling. So, there wound up being a whopping thirty-seven assembly points.

"You want us to do *what*?"

Complaints broke out from everywhere. The devised strategy was easier said than done. For those of us who had to actually orchestrate it, we now had thirty-seven times more work.

So you see what we were dealing with. It was certainly an unexpected scenario, but we'd prepared ourselves for any situation and weren't caught too off guard. Though swamped with work, we knew what to do. But just then, the Chief of Staff added a few conditions. You know what they were?

"Half of the Office of the Army Staff's Mobilization Planning Division has joined the coup and deserted their command posts."

Even a list of traitors was sent down to us. The message? Do your job with half as many people. The director of the Nonplan Room was on the list and oh my word, she walked out the room with a smirk. Those of us remaining were obviously in for a shit show. But the ones off the hook must've been jubilant. Couldn't the people who changed sides have practiced mobilizing for the insurgency? Of course not. What kind of army trains you to stage a coup? The insurgents just sat around chilling out.

The simulation ended in a baffling way, with the Chief of Staff committing suicide and the coup losing steam. Though we didn't pull off a crushing victory, we did manage to stop the coup one way or another. Our director got a National Medal for that, you know. The fact that we'd come up with some semblance of a plan in such a ridiculous situation must've impressed the higher-ups. And guess what they did for us? They downsized our Nonplan Room team by half. They said we seemed capable of doing our jobs with half the team. Geez.

At any rate, our jobs gave us a thorough education on elevators. We had to learn every single elevator line like doctors memorizing the names of bones. We often went on site visits too. We knew more about elevator lines than most Transportation Planning Division staff. We didn't just study elevator lines either. We also had to know pedestrian routes like the back of our hands. Our familiarity with back alleys matched that of Beanstalk's geography experts.

But once we realized that hard work only resulted in downsizing, everybody took it easy and often just went out and about on the pretense of doing site visits. No one felt guilty of course, and the higher-ups didn't seem to mind. After all, a situation in which the Nonplan Room had to step in wasn't very likely.

If a war really did break out, isn't it obvious what would happen? A defense line would be set up along the Level 22 border and more reservists would be enlisted. Training with the existing twenty-three mobilization plans was sufficient preparation.

Except trainings of that sort were not our job. We just had to be creative. The higher-ups wouldn't have been too happy if incompetent staff were lounging about, but we had proven ourselves already.

That was a period when we had too much free time and no work. And let me tell you, by then we'd gained a vast amount of geographic knowledge and had access to a shitload of information. If done right, we just might be able to have some fun with it. That's when the thought hit me: the woman next door. I'd been itching to know who lived on the other side of that wall for seven years. So, I did some digging. It wasn't very difficult to find out who she was.

She was a horizontalist. Not a half-baked one but a true fundamentalist. She'd co-authored a textbook on horizontalist economics and had been an activist for the Horizontal Culture Collective. At the time, she was mostly giving lectures with titles like "The Philosophical Implications of Horizontalist Ideology" or "The Horizontal-Economic Foundations of Skyscraper Capitalism." I went to her talks sometimes and zealously took notes.

How should I put this, her talks had a compassion to them. I knew this didn't necessarily mean every horizontalist was kindly, but her warmth struck a chord with me. Of course, I'm not saying I became a horizontalist. You think it's easy to become one? As for me, I wasn't about to go around introducing myself as a horizontalist when I hadn't even studied basic texts like *Vertical Capital*. Not that I had the desire to read the thing.

I just liked her. If she said something, I was persuaded. She published a book called *A Study on Level 520* the following year, and it might be the most beautiful work in the thirty-year history of horizontalism. She wrote what she'd observed during the seven years she lived on Level 520 and wrote purely from her own insights without relying on any horizontalist theory. The book literally just talks about Level

520 but, wow, to think that such a moving story could come out of that one floor—this meant there were over six hundred more such worlds in the rest of Beanstalk. That's why I couldn't help but nod at what the horizontalists were saying.

Also, the book mentions the exam-crammer neighborhood I used to live in. It tells stories about tenants who lost their homes to elevator redevelopment in the outskirts and contains little vignettes of the local horizontal labor union enjoying a picnic, and so on. Stories that held little meaning to people who didn't know the place but were riveting to those who did.

Maybe she and I had already met before. We wouldn't have recognized each other, but who knows, I could've bumped into her at the corner of a corridor somewhere, back when I was out looking for a job, trembling in the cold. In any case, I eventually found her.

She didn't know who I was yet. It seemed that my dutiful attendance of her lectures wasn't enough for her to recognize my face. I didn't tell her who I was, either, because I had no romantic intentions. But I wanted to thank her at least. Saying thanks wasn't too difficult. Besides, we did live in the same building.

But a new Chief of Staff was appointed around that time and spoiled my plan. The Mobilization Planning Division was merged with the Security Guardhouse's Transportation Planning Division and renamed the Strategic Planning Division. The division growing bigger wasn't an issue, but the head of the former Transportation Planning Division taking charge of performance evaluations was bad news for those of us from Mobilization Planning. Meaning, I had to stay at my desk during work hours again if I wanted to survive. Hectic days began and for a while I couldn't go see her. Just for a while.

The new Chief of Staff was off her rocker. The situations she gave us for maneuver exercises were a mess, for starters. I had no idea how to categorize them. Moreover, our merger with the Security Guardhouse's Transportation Planning Division dumped a whole load of rescue missions on our plates, which made me have second thoughts about my job. Why did I have to do this? Was the Transportation Planning Division leeching off our expertise to make their jobs easier? I bet that really was the case. And this integration of responsibilities would be the perfect excuse for the Chief of Staff to seize wartime operational control over the Security Guardhouse's combat teams.

Anyhow, we were a lot busier than we used to be. As if the heavier workload wasn't enough, the transportation people had zero experience with our line of work. It was a downright hassle to teach them on top of doing our own work.

The situation we were given for the maneuver exercise in the latter half of that year was a fire evacuation on Level 347. I was already in a demoralized, do-I-have-to-do-this state of mind when the division head called me in one day and told me out of nowhere to write a report.

When I asked, "What report?" the division head replied that he wanted an assessment on building an elevator exclusively for the mayor, one that ran directly from his office to the ground floor of Beanstalk. Chief of Staff's orders, apparently.

I said OK. What choice did I have? I wrote the report too, though the conclusion I drew was: "I don't think we need it."

For an elevator connecting the mayor's office to the ground floor, the price of land alone would be astronomical. I'd say it would cost as much as three fighter jets. Basically, the project had a very dubious return on investment. Pure verticalist thinking, if you ask me.

But the Chief of Staff was keen to push ahead with the project, thanks to which I became quite free again. That's the kind of organization the Beanstalk Army is. It assigns the least busy positions to the least competent or its least favorite personnel. On the bright side, I was assured of keeping my job, and as long as I showed no interest in getting promoted, I could carry on calling myself a government official, if only on paper, until full retirement age. I was secretly glad.

I started seeking out her lectures again. But her public appearances had grown noticeably rare in those last few months. I wondered what was going on, and I soon found out when I went to a few talks by other horizontalists. Folks were becoming more radical. They were awfully sensitive and aggressive. About what? This was when verticalist cartels were growing ever more powerful, mind you. The horizontalists were probably lashing out against that.

Since I'd been registered in a horizontal labor union once, some people recognized me at horizontalist talks. When I used to run into people I knew, we would greet each other like old buddies and banter for a bit, but not anymore. They had their guard up. Some people straight-up told me to leave the lecture hall. They thought I'd come to monitor them. I was a government official after all. And a known elevator expert at that.

So, I stopped going, but I couldn't bear to miss her talks. One day, I learned she was doing a talk on *A Study on Level 520* along with a book signing. How could I not go? I considered disguising myself but decided that would only look more suspicious, so I went as I was, holding my head up, my copy of *A Study* in hand.

When I went to get my copy signed after her lecture, lo and behold, she recognized me.

"It's you again," she said.

I felt compelled to defend myself. "Er, I know what this looks like, but I'm not a creep."

She smiled without saying anything. I was embarrassed. As she returned the signed book to me, she said, "There's a little debate club that I run, would you like to come by and give a talk sometime?"

"Pardon?"

"I can't give you much of a fee, I'm afraid. I'm scraping by myself, as you can see."

"It's not the fee I'm confused about ..."

"Ah, verticalism isn't exactly our group's strong suit, both theoretically and policy-wise. We'd like to invite an expert and learn. Please think about it and let me know."

When I opened the book, I found her contact information written inside. I wondered what had just happened. So, what did I do? What do you think? Can't say no to someone who saved my life, can I?

"It won't be a friendly debate," she said brightly when I

called five days later. "You might want to come prepared …"

"Don't worry," I assured her.

The seminar was as menacing as she had warned. I'm pretty sure I swore. Everyone else being academics, they knew how to throw shade without resorting to vulgar language, whereas I didn't have that gift at all. I swore within the first hour. I gathered up my things and stormed out. I received a call from her just as I got home.

"I'm sorry," I apologized.

But she said enthusiastically, "Sorry? You were amazing today!"

That's how we became friends. We had to meet in secret though. Why the secrecy? The era called for it. Things weren't so bad before, but people had grown increasingly polarized until it became very easy to tell a verticalist from a horizontalist.

But was it really such a black and white situation? I was fascinated by *A Study on Level 520*, yet someone like me was labeled a verticalist without question. And she was fascinated by my horror stories about elevator maneuver exercises. To me, the line between the two camps was blurry. It was a dotted line, and treading both sides of it didn't seem like such a huge deal, but verticalists wound up banning *A Study* in the military. Horizontalists were the same—they banned me from their lectures.

"Should we create 'diagonalism' or something?" I asked her once.

"Shall we?"

But neither of us were too perturbed. We went about our

business expecting the hubbub to die down eventually. I wasn't sorry that I was banned from lecture halls. As long as I got to see her, I was fine.

She and I only met up for the occasional late-night chat over coffee. Sometimes we had cocktails but never till we were drunk. We had enough fun sober.

"Do you know how to make a bomb?" I had asked her once.

"Obviously," she had replied.

"Not a Jägerbomb, a real bomb."

"What do you think?"

She was like that. She wasn't exactly the mild, gentle type. Perhaps she was dangerous. Not that she was a "person of interest" as verticalists like to say, but she made you feel a certain thrill. I mean, making a bomb only out of ingredients allowed in Beanstalk was not secret knowledge. Anyone could do it if they wanted to.

That's how we slowly got to know each other. One day she confided to me that she grew up in a pretty well-off family for a horizontalist, and I chortled to myself. I already knew, see. Someone who spent that much on heating couldn't have grown up poor.

I debated for a long time whether I should tell her about eight years ago but decided to keep the secret to myself. What do you mean, "Why?" I'd look like a loser. Plus, if I brought it up, I'd have to mention that I deliberately sought her out, which might make me look like a stalker.

That's all there was to us, even if our story might sound romantic. There was nothing serious going on between us but, wouldn't you know, strange gossip started circulating at some point. An executive board member or whatever of a horizontal labor union apparently saw us talking at a coffee shop by a Level 530 window. There was a rumor we were dating.

A junior co-worker told me about it and my response was, "So what?"

"You know there's going to be an uproar if the higher-ups find out," my co-worker replied.

"What uproar? Besides, you think they wouldn't know by now, if even you knew?"

The division head called me in to his office that afternoon. When I went, he asked if the rumor was true. "I heard you two have a kid already?" he asked.

"Excuse me?"

If *I* had it so bad, imagine how bad it must've been for her, because the rumor had started from her end. Of course, neither of us tended to care so much about these things, but over time they did get to me. She had always been on the moderate side of horizontalist theorists, but whenever she took a moderate stance, people suspected she'd backed down on my account. I was in the same boat. My stance was that vertical maneuvers using elevators can't achieve proper deployment on their own, remember? I'd been saying that long before I met her. Horizontal maneuvers were often more useful than vertical ones given Beanstalk's structure. But people weren't so keen to buy that argument anymore once the rumor about her spread.

Take the mayor's private elevator for instance. I recommended that instead, he build eight or so evacuation shelters with protective walls on the same floor as his office. Think about it. Then he could be evacuated to one of the eight shelters depending on the situation. Wouldn't that be much safer? The rest of the shelters could accommodate other people too. And most importantly, building eight of those cost far less than building one elevator that ran to the ground floor. The real estate costs alone would be, phew.

Anyway, that's how I lost touch with her. I thought it'd be best for the both of us. I didn't make a conscious decision to cut off contact; we slowly drifted apart. Not that I was overjoyed about it. We couldn't meet despite living in the same building—we'd gone back to how things were eight years ago in that we were so close, yet to reach each other we had to zigzag through the complex maze that was Beanstalk.

I was also busy with work. I'd been assigned to help with the maneuver exercises again—back to my real job. Up until then I'd been given extraordinarily little work for over half a year, maybe because that business over the mayor's private elevator had made me a marked man. From what I could tell, my bosses couldn't send me away to an entirely new division since I had expertise, but they were also reluctant to put me in charge of important work. Well, I didn't complain. All I had to do was teach junior personnel and handle administrative work. Not that admin was fun, but it was loads better than maneuver exercises. But those good days had come to an end.

There were two types of maneuver exercises at the time: exercises in the first half of the year focused on standard deployment training that followed a prearranged defense plan, those in the second half on war games involving contingencies. So, the first half shouldn't require very much practice, right? But that year's exercise included a situation that was unheard of. A mayor evacuation drill had been added in last minute. Evidently, the mayor's private elevator was finished.

The work itself wasn't hard. What was so hard about sending someone down a private elevator? All you had to do was press the ground floor button and shut the door. The hard part was protocol, you know? Seeing as the higher-ups had poured jillions of the national defense budget into the elevator, they would've wanted it to make a strong impression when it was unveiled. As it turned out, folks from the old Transportation Planning Division were talented in that department.

But they weren't up to scratch when it came to keeping confidentiality. The average citizen wouldn't have noticed, but experts like us knew a problem when we saw one. Like all long-distance elevators, the mayor's private elevator didn't descend in a straight vertical line but at sharp zigzags, according to which land was purchasable. That was much safer anyway in terms of security. But it was critical that they didn't leak the construction details when building a secret elevator like that. And they shouldn't leave any traces on the map once it was complete. The easiest solution would be to pretend they were doing maintenance work on existing elevator lines. In fact, they did buy a portion of existing lines for some segments. They had to if they wanted to speed up construction. My only gripe was their less-than-smooth execution. It was glaring even at first glance.

I was pretty friendly with one of the junior personnel who

used to be in the Transportation Planning Division. I had a bit of a guilty conscience when it came to him. When the Transportation Planning Division merged with us in the Mobilization Planning Division, he asked me how he could adjust quickly to the way things were done here, so I told him to proactively do as much legwork as possible, draft up proposals, and essentially become an employee that pesters the director. Then about two months later, the director said to me over drinks, "The kid's such a pain in the ass. I think he's a bit dim."

As a result he was nudged off the career ladder like me, which in turn resulted in our becoming friends. For my part, I was feeling apologetic. Anyway, I would give him advice on one thing or another sometimes, and that day was one such occasion.

"Hey, don't you think the security's a bit lax?" I asked the guy. "I can almost *see* where the mayor is passing through just by looking at this map."

Those words caused trouble. The words themselves didn't mean much, but later there was an incident that changed everything.

You know about the incident I'm talking about, right? The explosion. It happened around the time the maneuver exercises were wrapping up that year. A bomb went off in the center of Level 133. An attack during an exercise? It sent the whole Office of the Army Staff into a frenzy. No one had died but the point of the explosion was uncanny—right next to the mayor's private elevator line. And the timing was bad too, it was a very close shave. If the bomb went off just five minutes earlier the mayor would've met a violent death in the elevator, so really, it wasn't so much an accident as a terrorist attack.

That's why my words became problematic. The security guards accused horizontal-separatists of being behind the attack, you see. A few hardcore horizontalist groups were identified as suspects, including the one that woman belonged to. You know, the debate club where I gave a talk before. So, I was blamed for sharing the location of the mayor's private elevator with that crowd.

"You're under warrantless arrest for violating traffic secret laws."

No fewer than six security guards came to escort me.

They couldn't prove I was guilty, obviously. It wasn't a crime to give a talk there. Neither was my relationship to the woman. All they got out of their investigations were anticlimactic stories. Big surprise, we didn't do anything. Our platonic relationship didn't even involve handholding. What's funny is that there isn't a single article in Beanstalkian law defining such relationships. Turns out people who didn't have a physical relationship had no relationship at all, legally speaking. The Beanstalk Security Act, which was originally created for building management purposes, judges whether sex occurred by the occupancy of a room. Apparently, two people need to occupy the same private space over a certain period of time for their relationship to be deemed physical. But we hadn't done that. Ever.

A security guard asked, "What? There's nothing between you two. How did the rumors get so out of hand?"

"That's what I've been trying to tell you," I replied.

The security guards interrogated me for three whole days to reach that unremarkable conclusion. They didn't give me an especially hard time, but I was put in an awkward position all the same. Me, a spy?

It's not like I never suspected her. I don't know if they were telling the truth but the security guards said to me, "She as good as confessed. Your loss if you keep denying it."

I told them, "You don't seriously expect me to believe that, right?"

Despite saying that, I wasn't so confident. There was a good chance I'd been used. I *had* told her about the mayor's private elevator, though I hadn't revealed the exact location. But the security guards seemed to decide I wasn't worth investigating any further once they discovered that the rumor about me and her was blown out of proportion. They had plenty of other fish to fry.

I was released without drama and went back to my office, much to the division head's annoyance. You see, the Security Guardhouse's investigation team had concluded that even without an insider's tipoff, anyone could've easily located the mayor's private elevator just by studying the map a little carefully. It'd become clear how lax the security was. I'm sure the division head wasn't ecstatic about that.

My director was different, though. She probably knew me best as I'd worked with her since my days in the Mobilization Planning Division. She seemed to think this was actually a good opportunity to put me back on key projects. My heart was grateful but my body, I knew, would be exhausted from the work. Well, what could I do. I had to go with the flow. That's what it took to survive.

As work kept my body busy, my mind calmed. But with time, a corner of my heart felt empty again. Something had turned up in the investigations. She had a man. And a kid. That's how the rumor had gone around that the kid was mine.

I wondered if there'd truly been nothing between us, if I'd really been used. It was plausible, wasn't it? I myself couldn't trust our relationship anymore.

Meanwhile, investigations into the elevator terrorist attack began in earnest. Horizontalists were summoned one by one. Most of them turned out to be false alarms, but the security guards didn't mind so much. They seemed to be more interested in harassing the horizontalist camp than in solving the case.

So, it wasn't surprising that the horizontalists turned aggressive too. Some of them became level-separatists. It's true that level-separatism is the crux of horizontalist theory, but traditionally, separatists weren't hardliners. They just wanted the unique cultures of each level to be respected instead of being lumped together. There were, of course, groups that were extremist from the start, like the Level 72 Horizontal Labor Union or the Level 154 Day Laborers' Union, but these organizations were too disparate for them to integrate vertically. Maybe that was the innate limitation of horizontalists. Without a vertical coalition, they couldn't wield meaningful political power no matter how many of them there were.

But the separatists finally started joining forces as the horizontalists came under more and more pressure. "Separatist

Unity," can you imagine? It doesn't even make sense, but back then it really was a thing. Those separatists have no shame, do they? The Level 520 Labor Union jumped on board and that woman got involved too. As she was a very important theorist, she would've been forced to pick a side, right? *Don't give us an ambivalent attitude, either you're in or you're out.* I bet that's how it went down.

And I was tasked with cracking down on that lot. I didn't have any qualms though. Like I said, I didn't subscribe to any "-ism." My area of expertise just happened to be elevators, I never really cared what that entailed. Aren't most people like that? Sifting with a vertical sieve will only leave horizontalists, just as sifting with a horizontal sieve will only leave verticalists. When in fact most people can be sifted both ways.

But at the time it was more advantageous to wear the mask of a v-winger for my own safety, and I wore it unapologetically. I did it to survive. She probably did the same as a h-winger, too, to survive with her integrity intact among other h-wingers. But did we truly make the right choice? No one gave us the answer to that. No one probably knew the answer.

That's how "Plan 24" was formed. We'd received intelligence that Cosmomafia may be behind the elevator terrorist attack—the formula for making highly explosive bombs had apparently been brought in by outside forces. Since we had twenty-three wartime mobilization plans, Plan 24 was a show of commitment to treat the fight against terrorism as a wartime situation. The plan actually involved mobilizing the security guards instead of the Army, but that didn't make a huge difference.

The plan's key purpose was to empower the security guards, during emergencies, to requisition the forty-four new long-distance elevator lines built mostly in the city's outskirts. That way the security guards could close in on the enemy pretty much from all sides no matter where the conflict was.

The idea was fairly simple, right? But as even long-distance elevators didn't connect all the floors of Beanstalk, transfers were again the problem. So, it wasn't that simple in practice. Not many people were qualified to execute it, making the pool of candidates for Plan 24 Control Room duties obvious. Maybe three people including me? Plan 24 was practically thrust into my hands. The director of the Nonplan Room was technically in charge, but she was too busy dealing with transportation companies in the Vertical Transportation Cooperative to study elevator lines.

The attempted elevator bombing case didn't look like it'd be solved anytime soon. The security guards still had no leads on the perpetrators. But the City Council went ahead and passed the Long-distance Elevator Ordinance Amendment Bill to execute Plan 24. The Council must've thought that an emergency response organization was necessary now that a bomb had appeared, never mind who planted it. So when seventy local horizontal labor unions affiliated with Separatist Unity all went on strike that weekend to protest the coming crackdown, it wasn't an overreaction, if you ask me. That's how this business escalated into a full-scale crisis.

Be that as it may, I decided to just focus on doing my job. When the higher-ups gave orders, I moved the security guards as instructed, simple. What was there to think about?

Plan 24 commenced, and I was transferred to the Plan 24 Control Room as planned. A "situation" hadn't occurred yet, and the director was tracking down vertical transportation companies and badgering them to empty the elevators immediately. That job was no picnic since business owners weren't always a kindly bunch. The owners insisted on running their businesses as usual until a situation occurred. I bet it wouldn't have been easy to persuade them before anything happened. I'm not saying their insistence was justified; the elevators weren't built with their money alone. The city government had paid a sizable share. It had a perfect right, in other words, to requisition the elevators *before* a situation arose. That was the condition on which the project had received government funding in the first place.

The director and the business owners were still at it when the Security Guardhouse briefed me on how the guards were currently deployed. Unlike the military, the security guards weren't clustered around the border. They were spread all over Beanstalk already, so I didn't need to move a huge number of guards in one direction. The other side was the same; all seventy local horizontal labor unions weren't assembled in one place. I didn't have to worry about bottlenecks.

The hard part was deploying the right number of guards to the most urgent area as conditions changed. I also had to carefully choose assembly points that would allow guards to surround the union members with ease the moment they were needed. Plan 24 was, in that sense, impossible to plan in advance. What with also having to think up civilian evacuation plans on the spot, it was more like "Nonplan 24." But then the budget for it was disproportionately huge, and if that were exposed, more than one or two heads would roll. Hence why these people had no choice but to rely on me to make a nonplan look like a plan. It was time for me to show off my skills.

Then, a situation arose at last. There'd been intelligence that horizontal labor unions had started marching. Of course, it wasn't my job to assess how things stood. The Security Guardhouse Situation Room was responsible for that. I simply had to swiftly move guards as I'd been ordered to. Two teams to District F on Level 170, four teams to District G on Level 319, then one tactical unit to District A on Level 489, and so on.

"One tactical unit? You want us to assemble it at A57 on Level 487? What's at A57?" Looking nonplussed, our director sometimes asked the Security Guardhouse Situation Room to confirm if it gave us the right order, but I never felt the need to do that myself. I was just a well-oiled machine. I could be an evil weapon if misused, but I believed the work I was doing was good.

I could tell things were tense at the Security Guardhouse Situation Room as reports arrived one after another of people claiming to have seen explosives. People have a tendency to witness nonexistent bombs in times of unrest, you know. Those days were like that—a time when reports of bomb threats came in daily. But I kept getting orders from above to move our forces to meaningless spots. The higher-ups were clearly ruffled. I didn't contradict them. Nor did the director.

The situation was unpredictable. I'd come under fire if an action I took on my own initiative resulted in casualties.

When I received the order to relocate three tactical units of guards to Level 520, I knew the moment had come. That was where the woman was. But no matter. She had nothing to do with me. I was reconfiguring the elevator network when the first bomb exploded.

Well, it was the worst situation I'd ever encountered. Beanstalk's border control was supposed to be so strict that you could safely assume it was impossible to smuggle in a bomb. A proper bomb, that is. Damaging the building structure with fire or explosives is a serious crime, just below actual insurrection. That's because Beanstalk began as a building, not a nation. Anyway, a bomb not smuggled across the border was likely homemade, and the first one to go off that day was astonishingly potent for a homemade bomb. That must've been the new technology brought in from Cosmomafia. I suddenly remembered what the woman once told me.

"Do you know how to make a bomb?" I had asked.

"Obviously," she had replied.

"Not a Jägerbomb, a real bomb."

"What do you think?"

"I know how to make one too."

"It isn't enough to make one. It has to detonate well. Very well, in fact."

A defiance rose in me. I thought: alright, bring it on then.

The military stepped in soon after the bomb went off. As if it'd been preparing for that moment. The timing was suspicious, but it may have just been the military being competent.

I was fine with it stepping in, except the Strategic Planning Division started requisitioning elevators. Oh, that drove me nuts. If an elevator I'd just sent up was somehow down on Level 25, what the heck was I supposed to do?

The business owners were just as confused. They phoned nonstop. "Whose damn order do you want us to follow?" The director must've had a horrible time too. She couldn't tell them to listen only to her, since she was originally from the Strategic Planning Division.

The elevator lines became a hot mess in no time. Military troops were mixed up with security guards in more and more locations. Something had to be done. I decided to sort out the chain of command first and was making calls all over the place when *BOOM!* The second bomb went off.

"You (*bleep*)s! What the (*bleep*) are you doing?"

It'd taken exactly one minute for my phone to start ringing off the hook. The callers hurled obscenities at me, but even the obscenities lacked a single chain of command, the same expletives pouring in from everywhere.

First, I became the offspring of a dog, then was an illegitimate child, then a piece of excrement, and later even a toad. All this colorful language streamed in through three telephone lines, which of course rendered the communication network dysfunctional.

If only my father hadn't speculated in that satellite, I wouldn't have been subjected to such humiliation! It was the first time I thought that, you know. But what could I do? The past is the past. I had to put out the fire at my heels first, right?

Just then I spotted an elevator being sent toward a fire station. It threw me for a second, but I resolved to leave it be. Instead, I opted for a turn-based strategy since controlling every single elevator using a real-time strategy felt like a stretch. I intended to halt all elevators first, then move only the elevators that were done running. The Strategic Planning Division seemed to cotton on to my plan before long. Though slower than moving all elevators simultaneously, this approach was better than having the chain of command completely mixed up.

Well, it still got mixed up at one point. A group of elevators moving simultaneously came out of nowhere, you see. A third party had intervened: the Vertical Transportation Cooperative, I later learned, had independently started controlling lines to supply twenty elevators for civilian evacuation. But at the time, neither the Strategic Planning Division nor the Plan 24 Control Room had been informed of the fact. How were we supposed to know there was a third party in the picture? Each assumed that the other had broken the agreement.

So, the elevator lines got messed up again. A bedlam if there ever was one. We were grappling with the ruckus when for the third time, a bomb erupted. We received another round of calls from above, another shower of insults.

We were copulators, then we were the heads of male organs.

We came to our senses thanks to profanities taking the place of commands: the director phoned up the Vertical Transportation Cooperative and showered it with commands in the new language. Clarity was restored to the system. Stop all elevators first. Don't touch moving elevators. Move stationary elevators immediately.

The crisis eased at once. Elevators were finally serving their function. A bomb is obviously dangerous, but at the end of the day it's only a tactical weapon that serves a limited purpose. Unless designed for mass destruction, a weapon usually can't win against strategy. If you look at it that way, elevators make a more powerful instrument of war than bombs. A bomb is a trifle, really.

Of the seventy local horizontal labor unions, I suspected ten at most were radical enough to use bombs. The rest weren't that dangerous. Those ten unions weren't very difficult to overpower, either, since their forces weren't concentrated in one place. The trick was to besiege each district with a small number of guards first and move the main, larger body of guards to arrest the leaders, district by district. It was only when every other district was suppressed that I finally sent guards to Level 520. By then I just wanted to do my job and get it over with.

Truly dangerous things happen at such moments, right? When everybody's guard is down. The fourth bomb went off.
BOOM!
The noise was deafening. It didn't travel through the air but through the building. The boom sounded not just from above and below but from everywhere. Then, I heard something collapse as if an earthquake had struck.

That was the strongest bomb to detonate that day, strong enough to shake the whole building. We paused our work from shock, and the elevators paused automatically too, thinking it was an earthquake.

I waited to be bombarded with phone calls, but none came. The situation seemed bad—clearly, it was no time for showers of curses. The explosion was deadlier than anyone had imagined. I bet nobody knew a homemade bomb could be that deadly. By Beanstalkian standards, this bomb was of such force it could be considered a strategic weapon.

Most significantly though, the bomb had exploded on Level 520 of all places. The beautiful floor described in *A Study on Level 520*. I didn't have the details yet from intelligence, but I could roughly guess what happened. The only radical labor union that hadn't been suppressed yet was the one on Level 520.

The shaking stopped, and the instant I was sure the building wouldn't collapse, my heart sank. The woman! Her face flashed across my mind. The one person I still knew who lived on Level 520.

No, this isn't right! This isn't how it should have gone!

The maneuver exercises were to blame. Doing them for years made us think this was some game—we mistook them for playing with toy soldiers. We thought we were playing advanced chess on a three-dimensional chessboard. We couldn't have been more smug about it too. It was an uncommon skill after all. But in that moment, I couldn't help wringing my hands over what I'd done. I was suddenly scared.

Of course, I personally hadn't done anything. I hadn't called the shots. I'd only done what I was told. That's what I kept telling myself. But that and all else became meaningless the instant a tremor from that fourth explosion rippled through the Plan 24 Control Room. Now wasn't the moment to debate such matters, not when the explosion was violent enough to rock the entire building.

I phoned the Security Guardhouse Situation Room, but now *their* line was engaged. The bomb had destroyed everything within a fifty-meter radius, leaving hundreds of people dead or injured. Utter catastrophe. But those figures were much smaller than what our commanders had initially anticipated. We'd expected the damages to be more extensive given the staggering magnitude of the shock.

Unsurprisingly, Emergency Evacuation Plan No. 1 took effect ten minutes later. It was a contingency plan for emptying the whole of Beanstalk. A plan for all 500,000 of the population to escape to the neighboring country. I kid you not. The order was issued and everything. We honestly had thought the whole building would collapse. We bureaucrats were overreacting out of guilt.

It was the emergency of emergencies. How in the world were we supposed to evacuate 500,000 people? But the order had been issued and we had to act. The Strategic Planning Division made the first move, sounding the siren and forcing civilians to evacuate.

What was it like? Mayhem is what it was. A riot could break out any minute. There weren't enough elevators, but hordes of people had to get out, so the Strategic Planning Division must've thought that clearing the floors from bottom to top was the reasonable course of action. Thing is, people on the lower floors weren't in such a hurry. The bomb had exploded on Level 520. People in the upper-level districts were naturally more desperate.

People below were dawdling, people above were scrambling to get down. Eventually a brouhaha erupted in the Level 200s. That caused quite the chaos for us in the Plan 24 Control Room too, since we had to send all the security guards to those levels. Civilians were stirring up their own rumpus claiming that the security guards were sent down before them, while the higher-ups were calling in to ask if they could be evacuated first. In what was the craziest uproar we'd ever laid eyes on, we had only managed to evacuate twenty-thousand people before another brouhaha broke out down below.

Do you think the neighboring country sat around watching twenty-thousand people suddenly cross their border? The endless outpouring of Beanstalkians turned the roads and surrounding area into a complete mess. And you know that native Beanstalkians have absolutely no real sense of what a road is, right? So, they just spilled out onto the roads. The neighboring country's government had to blockade Beanstalk. It was basically telling Beanstalkians to stop coming outside. That was the obvious course of action when people were crossing into its land without permission. Not just any people but Beanstalkians, who'd been notoriously strict with border checks.

By then the Beanstalkian government had no other choice than to continue the evacuation. Once people started being pushed down towards the exits, there was no way to push them back up. They flooded down from above only to be blocked below. What could the government do? Push through by brute force. The Army was ordered to mobilize and dismantle the barricade set up by the neighboring country's police. Think about it: that's essentially ordering an attack.

By the time fifty-thousand people had poured out, the neighboring country's military was mobilized too. Beanstalk, in turn, ordered a partial mobilization of reserve forces since our army was smaller in size—a "war" was about to break out. It was a hair-trigger moment that, thankfully, didn't lead to engagement. The situation had only escalated that far in the confusion, and the neighboring country knew perfectly well that we had no intention of invading it.

When about eighty-thousand people had crossed the border, the neighboring country's government made an official announcement. Apparently, it was granting Beanstalkians refugee status in the spirit of humanitarianism. Moving its line of defense back slightly, it declared the area around Beanstalk a refugee camp. I'm sure it was being remunerated by Beanstalk in return.

And so people cascaded down. All told, 457,000 people fled across the Level 22 border. The only ones remaining inside were rescue workers or security guards who absolutely had to stay. I think I heard that a stray dog was running around Level 487, believe it or not. Anyway.

I also escaped the building by dawn. It was surprisingly cold. An almost midwinter chill had struck even though it was early spring. What a spectacle I saw downstairs. Droves of humans thrown out onto the street without warning, stretching endlessly along the pavement. I really couldn't see where the crowd ended, even though people were jam-packed together.

Just then, a blast of wind blew and everyone shrieked. We were cold. Cold enough to freeze to death. Most of us had run out without a decent coat. We didn't know it was that cold outside.

Everyone was shivering in the same wind, all of us at the same altitude. We gazed up at Beanstalk all night. Shrieking in unison at every gush of wind, prompting the neighboring country's police to yell at us to shut up.

Who knew the phrase could be so hurtful? I teared up in indignation. But you know what, I wasn't the only one feeling that way. We'd filled the streets, tightly, and could feel each other's thoughts through the skin. A realization dawned on me in that instant.

Oh, we're all thinking the same thing!

It was a strange realization. The kind where you even realize that everyone else realized what you realized.

The wind blew. *Eeeeeek*! A shriek rang out. *Eeeeeek*! Another shriek sounded from elsewhere like an echo. The *eeeeek*'s followed the direction of the wind and swelled towards me like a great wave. *Eeeeeek*!

In the heart of that great wave, we shed hot tears. And all of us looked up at Beanstalk. The realization dawned on us: that tower must never fall! The realization that all 450,000 people were coming to the same realization gripped my heart again, hard.

And in that split-second the image of the woman flickered before my eyes. The memory kept coming back. The warmth radiating from my neighbor's room in days long gone when I'd almost frozen to death, the trace of life that had seeped through the wall.

That was love. The most devoted, absolute love. Similar to this unconditional love I was feeling towards the people currently shrieking the same shriek with me, my next-door neighbors. I wanted to see her.

I ran back to Beanstalk. As I rushed into the building, I was stopped by security guards.

"I'm a Strategic Planning Division agent!" I flashed my ID card and entered. Crossing the Level 25 border, I went up to the elevator terminal.

"Strategic Planning!" I held out my ID again and got onto an elevator.

"Excuse me sir, where are you going?" a security guard asked.

"The site of the explosion," I replied.

It occurred to me only then that I'd lost my old home. Level 520, a beautiful place I could never trade for another floor. The site of the explosion didn't even exist. A massive void had replaced it. A blackhole.

The emergency evacuation order was lifted the following day. What an embarrassing morning. After 450,000 of us had experienced the intimacy of screaming ourselves hoarse together, the general sentiment was like that of lovers who, after committing adultery all night and narrowly escaping the motel just before checkout time, were looking up at the midday sun with naked eyes.

It was later discovered that the bomb set off on Level 520

was not smuggled in from Cosmomafia but internally manufactured, meaning outside forces hadn't been involved. This had been a problem that arose within Beanstalk: a social problem, not a military one. It was an embarrassing morning in many ways.

Maybe that's why the influx of 450,000 people into the building was, compared to the previous day's chaos, remarkably peaceful. It was the best maneuver exercise ever. Zero hiccups.

I couldn't find the woman. Actually, I couldn't even try. All of Level 520 had been blasted away. Her name was on the list of missing people released two days later. That was all. Her body was never found.

I didn't know that I would be so calm the moment I read her name on the list. A thought crossed my mind: it wasn't my turn to grieve yet. There'd been nothing between me and her, after all. I must've perceived that I still had to wait for many others to grieve first before my turn came.

My turn did come in the end, no less than twenty years later. I was at a bookstore waiting for someone when a strange book caught my eye. The second I saw it my heart clenched and I couldn't compose myself. On the one hand, I even felt a little hurt that it had taken so long for my turn to come.

Can you guess what the title of the book was? *A Study on Level 217*. It was a heart-stoppingly beautiful book. On reading it, my thirty-year career felt like a stupid stunt. It had a voice strikingly similar to hers, but I don't know if she really wrote it, hiding somewhere in Beanstalk. I never checked. I didn't want to dig any further. I wanted to let it be.

Y'all are looking at me like "The old coot's giving us a useless lecture again." I'm just telling you the story because I was reminded of old times, hearing you folks are going to total war with Cosmomafia. I encourage you to ask yourselves if Cosmomafia is truly the cause of all your problems. Well, I guess you don't have much of a choice since you say the higher-ups have already decided to fight. Let me know if there's anything the Security Guardhouse can help with.

By the way, the Emergency Evacuation Plan No. 1 is impossible to execute now so don't even think about attempting it. The neighboring country won't have it. Just make sure a long-range missile doesn't land on Beanstalk, whatever it takes. Or else everybody'll wind up dead.

When will these goddamn wars end, anyway?

The Buddha of the Square

Sister-in-law,

Homeless? Come off it. I've never slept at a train station. I don't know who it was that you saw "looking like they'd completely given up on life," but that couldn't have been me.

As a matter of fact, I got a job. There was an opening for a security guard in Beanstalk. I couldn't tell you earlier because no one was around to listen—your sister had gone off on a business trip with the air of someone leaving for good. I was shocked but I didn't despair. Although I did feel the need to do something. Soon. Otherwise I didn't think I would ever get back on my feet.

And then I was completing my training, preventing me from contacting you this whole time. I'm required to live in isolation for the next little while. The Security Guardhouse here launched a new mounted horse unit, and the horses and riders are training together. In full military fashion.

Of course, I don't think the job particularly suits a long-time office worker like me. That's why I was very hesitant to take it, but it didn't turn out to be so bad once I started. The Beanstalk Security Guardhouse is essentially the police here after all, despite the name.

I've written to your sister, too, but she seems to have no intention of replying. I would appreciate it if you can put in a good word for me.

I can't write long because I'm in the middle of training. Well, please write back.

Brother-in-law,

Mounted guards galloping around a 674-floor building when I can't even imagine cars driving around there? And in a security guardhouse at that? I've asked around and discovered that you got the job through what's-his-name, Gwangdeuggie or some other thuggish name. Why have you been associating with him when you know my sister hates him? Did he also introduce you to those loan sharks you borrowed from as well? We *are* family, you know. Please tell me everything there is to tell. I'd like to help where I can.

My sister is staying at my house these days, as yours is in chaos due to your debt situation. She would not have gotten your letter if you sent it there. I doubt she would've read it even if she were there, judging by her lack of curiosity when I told her I'd received a letter from you.

She doesn't let on, but she is very worried about you. I heard that the place you got into is not the Beanstalk Guardhouse but some private security guard company. My sister asked if it isn't a group of thugs for hire, but I told her no, things in Beanstalk would be different from our country. But I wasn't too sure myself.

Please give us a call. I don't know what your situation is, but hearing you explain in your own voice will put us at ease.

Sister-in-law,

I'm not lying. I really am in the mounted horse unit. I work for a security firm specializing in security dogs, and they're launching a mounted unit for the first time. To tell you the truth, we only have ten horses and the rest are dogs, but the smell of the stable, if nothing else, is real, I assure you. If I am telling a lie and there is no mounted unit here, then how can you explain the vast amount of dung I cleaned this morning? I'll concede on everything else but not that!

We just got an elephant, and I have a feeling I'll be in charge of the fella. Apparently, nobody else has seen an elephant before because there are no zoos here. Everyone is irrationally scared of him. Not that I'm any good with elephants, but folks here seem to think I'm suited for the job. Elephants look much bigger inside Beanstalk, since they fill up a whole corridor. People here don't seem to have a realistic sense of his actual size as they've never seen an elephant outdoors. They're overwhelmed just by looking at him.

I know my story sounds strange, but that is what happened. I intend to stay here awhile. It would be best if I don't call. The loan sharks are listening in. And this way, I won't be a burden to you or your sister. I will write often, so for now please be patient.

I've written to your sister a few times, too, but she hasn't replied. Is she even reading my letters? Maybe she hasn't opened them because I sent them disguised as bills. Anyway, you're the best. Please fill her in for me.

Brother-in-law,

Did you go all the way to Beanstalk just to clean stables? You're not Sun Wukong in *Journey to the West*, you know. Brother-in-law, please don't pretend to punish yourself. Do you think that will mollify my sister? You should consider how we feel about what you're doing.

I read about your mounted security unit in the news. About how it was created to quell protests. I'm not sure what is going on exactly, but I don't think it's prudent to be involved in another country's affairs as a foreigner. I read that last year your company caused the death of a protestor, and the Beanstalk Security Guardhouse denied any responsibility. What if you get caught up in a situation and get hurt? It seems like the only one prosecuted last time was an employee from your company. Do be careful. It's OK to quit if you get cold feet.

Sending in security guards on horses to subdue a protest frankly sounds dangerous. It isn't something you are cut out for either. I know you're not that sort of person. I worry the experience might scar you.

Sister-in-law,

I think you've got the wrong idea—our horses are gentle. It's true that the mounted horse unit is for protest control purposes, but we have no plans to trample people. You know, countries like America have mounted police too.

The security guards here are ridiculously outnumbered by protestors. The guards used to manage the crowds by implementing a close order formation, but it doesn't seem to work very well anymore. You know what a close order formation is, right? The thing where you huddle together holding plastic shields to stand your ground. Civilians are normally intimidated just by the sight of ranks of uniforms and helmets, but these days the protestors apparently form a phalanx of their own. I guess professional protestors must have been recruited externally. Although civilians aren't as disciplined as the security guards, there are a lot more of them. When protestors intentionally set themselves up in an area from which they can't retreat in a win-or-die effort, they often smash through the security guards' lines. Casualties can happen then.

That's why the mounted unit was introduced. Civilians, unless they have especially strong discipline, probably won't withstand a mounted unit charge. If two tight rows of five horses rush toward the protestors, the five hundred people gathered in City Hall Square would scatter at once. That way we can prevent a direct confrontation. Of course, it'd be a different story if the protestors keep their close order formation and receive the charge, but I doubt that would ever happen. Why do you think the Middle Ages lasted over a thousand years in Europe? Because nobody had ever stood still when a cavalry was charging at them. What we're doing here is all based on calculations by experts. We're also training so that the mounted unit has to halt if protestors don't dodge out of the way until the last moment. The mounted unit would be useless if that moment arrives, but it won't. It would take a thousand years for a person with no professional military training to face a mounted unit charge head on.

So this is not unethical work. It's simply meant to forestall unnecessary conflicts. I won't get scarred.

I'm due at an assembly again now. I will write later. Bye now.

Brother-in-law,

You said it would take a thousand years. It didn't even take a hundred days. What did I tell you? Professional protestors, my foot! They didn't back off even when the mounted guards charged at them. The papers said so too—that they wouldn't have risked their lives and stood their ground until the last moment if they really were hired protestors. Anyone can see that this is a legitimate anti-war protest. The whole world knows Beanstalk and Cosmomafia are at war—it's no use pretending that you don't know.

So please, Brother-in-law, don't think of your work as playing with toy soldiers. Those people must have desperate reasons. I doubt they are protesting for fun. You never know what will happen if a real confrontation breaks out with such people. Also, a company like yours doesn't hire a foreigner like you for no reason. And an elephant on top of that? This is worrying.

Sister-in-law,

Thank you for your concern, but I will have to stay here for some time because the elephant was assigned to me. And the training period has been slightly extended. The higher-ups are hounding us to use the elephant in actual combat. They don't seem to have any alternatives. They can't use tear gas since everything is indoors, nor can they shoot water from the fire sprinklers in the square's ceiling, which is against fire safety regulations. They have to somehow break up the protestors' close order formation to suppress them, but it's not like they can bring in tanks or fire guns in a place like this.

My company is a right Carthaginian army these days. The higher-ups say the only solution is to do exactly what people used to do two thousand years ago: shields, clubs, and elephants. I feel like I've been recruited by General Hannibal, not Beanstalk. A Hannibal whose cavalry has lost its effectiveness.

By the way, this darned elephant generates so much poop. I bet he poops more than ten horses combined. Sometimes I wonder if I'm working for a janitorial service. It feels like my bosses procured an elephant especially for me in case I run out of things to clean.

This elephant fella, he's gentle but not very bright. Aren't elephants supposed to be smarter than horses? Because he didn't fit in an elevator, he was carried up with a tower crane from outside the building and that must've freaked him out. The sedative wore off midway so there was a big fuss shooting him with the tranquilizer gun again and all. He was so agitated he was crapping in heaps, phew. Just the thought of it kills my appetite.

Anyway, it seems we should meet up at least once, seeing how you're so worried. Since I can't leave here for the time being, would you could come by with your sister some time? You'd both be more at ease once you see for yourselves how I work. My job isn't as dangerous as you might think.

I wrote the same thing to your sister but still no news from her. Do try to persuade her. I always knew your sister was stubborn as a mule, but I'm only fully realizing it now.

Childish Brother-in-law,

I am not responsible for your and my sister's happiness. Not when I'm barely keeping myself afloat. You should've done better from the beginning. Who's the one that dragged you both into this mess?

The way I see it, you two are the same. My sister said what you said, suggesting she pop by Beanstalk. I told her to do as she pleased, and she asked me to accompany her. I said she should at least set up an appointment with you if we were going, but *that* she refused to do. Essentially, she wanted me to do it for her—you two really are the same.

Give me a date that works for you. I will coordinate accordingly.

Also, I wish you wouldn't include gross details in your letters. Your stories have got to be the most unpleasant of all the stories I've heard about Beanstalk. I don't know if Beanstalk is gross or you are.

As for even using an elephant in these circumstances, I don't know. It seems a little extreme? Brother-in-law, how about you get a job at a zoo instead?

My prim and proper sister-in-law,

I think around the XXth would be a good time to visit. The week before or after works as well. My schedule isn't fixed yet, but please help us set a time. Mediating between us must be a hassle, but that is what comes with being a sister-in-law. What choice do you have when you were born a sister? Patiently fulfilling your role will have its reward one day.

Your sister will understand everything once she sees me on the job. I did share unpleasant details, but this is, in fact, quite specialized work you know. People gape up at me when I sit impressively on the elephant and patrol the city. It's true. Some people may stare with curiosity, but I definitely feel there is something more. Admiration, perhaps? Of Amitabh obviously. That's the name of our elephant.

Amitabh is a nice fellow. He has the kindest eyes. He is *too* gentle, if anything. Why, minus the fact that he's huge and strong, he acts exactly like a puppy. He's good at recognizing people, and those flappy ears of his, oh he's a dear. Someone told me he used to follow Buddhist monks around, but as they were fasting all the time, they couldn't feed him properly and eventually handed him over to a zoo. They thought he had the temperament of a Bodhisattva.

The trouble is he's also such a scaredy-cat. I guess all animals are. Horses are apparently more easily frightened than humans, so they need rigorous training to be able to subdue a human. Elephants are the same. Although Amitabh is the first elephant I've ever taken care of, he certainly seems more faint-hearted than horses. But he really shouldn't be. If protestors realize he's scared, they may provoke him on purpose. The mere ring of a mobile phone makes him jump, which in turn makes *us* jump, in case we get stepped on by accident. This is some delicate profession, wouldn't you say?

Also, being an elephant, he can't walk just anywhere. He can only walk on floors reinforced to distribute weight, otherwise they might give way. As protests nearly always happen at the Level 321 square in front of City Hall, he just needs to make his way to and through the square. So, we lined the reinforced path with flowers to guide him. Perhaps that's why the negative public reaction to using an elephant for protest control has turned around. People seem intrigued. Some come just to see the elephant. Most people here have never seen one since, again, Beanstalk has no zoo.

Whenever we do a maneuver exercise at City Hall Square, young parents pushing strollers actually set up camp along the flower path. Now that makes us anxious to death. As much as we love that Amitabh has recovered from his ordeal, watching him sniff flowers as he moseys distractedly along the crimson flower path is downright nerve-racking. Nevertheless, I feel more at peace somehow on days I've taken Amitabh on a walk. Peering into his large, slowly blinking eyes, I think he's one ugly fella, but then a corner of my heart warms up. I feel more relaxed. Perhaps because he has such a slow gait. Watching him puts me in a daze.

Other people seem to get dazed too. When I look down from the elephant, I see people staring up at me, open-mouthed. An elephant must appear much more massive to locals than to you or me. I think that will be a big help in real situations. And they wouldn't be overly scared since by now everyone knows Amitabh is a gentle giant.

The mayor seems keen to piggyback on Amitabh's popularity. Whenever anything good happens, the man loves to brag that he's done it too. This time, he's claiming to have sponsored some wildlife rescue association in Africa for fifteen years and that he was always a true-blue elephant person or whatever. Amitabh is actually an Indian elephant.

Anyhow, you're in for a good show when you come visit. While loads of people come to watch Amitabh, many also come to people-watch. I'm something of a celebrity myself. Perhaps your sister will change her mind when she sees me at it. She'd realize that this guy isn't just loafing around somewhere.

Come over on a weekend around the date I mentioned. Please decide on a good day with your sister.

Brother-in-law,

I really don't know what to say.

I saw pictures of you online. The ones of you in City Hall Square or whatever you call it were OK as the ceiling is high there, but the ones taken elsewhere were ridiculous. You were hanging off the elephant, nearly squashed under the low ceiling, while people looked on in pity. And what's up with the uniform? You're not in a circus.

My sister is not impressed with your "clowning around." She says she'll pretend not to know you when you are riding the elephant. Attracting attention with such stunts won't make you a great person. People aren't looking at you in envy, they're looking because you're a spectacle. While I am glad you've gotten your confidence back, I think this has gone too far. If we come to see you, please don't plan on making your entrance like some ring master.

Also, we are not going all the way there just to see an elephant, and I doubt my sister will be moved even if she sees him. I don't buy your argument. No matter how you sugarcoat it, what you're doing seems unethical. How can anyone think of setting an elephant on protestors? It's incomprehensible to us, as is the fact that you're proud of your job or that locals marvel at the sight. I resent that the public's anti-war sentiments are being stamped out like that in the first place. Beanstalk may be swanky on the outside, but it's downright totalitarian.

As for your financial blunder, my sister made desperate pleas here and there and managed to sort out most of the mess. I have never seen her act so humble. You know how she is, right? If you keep up this cavalier attitude of yours, you might find it difficult to ever fully repair your relationship with my sister, even if you two make up later.

My sister and I won't cater to your schedule and visit on a weekend—we plan to take leave on a weekday and stay at a resort. We heard the new one by the south window on Level 410 is pretty good. I will send you the details later. See you then. Please contact me if anything comes up.

And Brother-in-law, you can use the phone now. Let's just call each other. It would save everyone a lot of trouble.

Sister-in-law,

I can't go home yet, if truth be told. Those bastards are watching me. You see, I didn't just borrow money from them. It would be safer for me to stay isolated as I am now. Phoning doesn't feel quite secure either. Let's stick to letters for now.

I feel more comfortable with letters after months of being cut off from the conveniences of civilization. And you know me, I blurt out nonsense whenever I open my mouth. Plenty of what I say can be misunderstood even in writing, but I sound marginally better this way. Also, let's say I called your sister. She'd swear at me within five minutes.

I can't tell swearing from speaking nowadays since I hear the former day in and day out. Half of the words I hear are swearwords. Maybe it's the people in this business. Sometimes I wonder if it's wise to stay in a place like this, as you pointed out. I might have quit a long time ago if it weren't for Amitabh.

Our elephant has become especially sweet-tempered lately. He was originally like that, according to the person who brought him from India. She was horrified when I told her he was hoisted up to Level 321 by a tower crane. She said he should've at least been put in a shipping container that he couldn't see outside of—how could anyone just tie rope around his body and haul him up? She said no elephant would be OK after suffering such treatment. That method was chosen for safety reasons though. It's not like there was a custom-made container for him, and a container carrying him could tilt, which would be disastrous. It could crash into the building wall. But an elephant would have no way of knowing that.

And folks here are clueless when it comes to heights— they have no fear. I've seen Beanstalkians lean out the window on Level 600 and stare down from it, none of them looking scared, young or old. People at my company must have thought an elephant wouldn't be scared either. Of course that didn't turn out to be true. Also, I bet they weren't sure how much tranquilizer was needed to put Amitabh to sleep because he was the first real elephant they had seen. Imagine his shock when he woke up dangling in midair.

But he seems to have calmed down over time. He can walk by himself now. I spend hours every day with him, and sometimes I can't help but think that he is not only gentle but also *sacred* somehow. My mind can't be more at peace when I stroll slowly by his side. Maybe I will reach enlightenment one of these days. I feel like a totally different person. A bit more reverent, if you will.

You'll see when we meet. See you then. Come to the fountain in City Hall Square on Level 321 at nine o'clock. I might be slightly late as I'll be washing the elephant. You have to wait for me, OK?

Brother-in-law,

Please come to your senses. Do you think any old person can reach enlightenment? Someone like you certainly can't. Frankly, I think you're running away from reality. My sister won't eat you alive, so please stop indulging in escapist fantasies. By all means, enlighten yourself if you want, but I wish you would set things in order before you do. After that you can become the Buddha or the Dalai Lama for all I care.

I heard there will be some kind of rally on the day we are meeting. Will we be OK? Should we reschedule? Please phone if possible. We're getting close to the date.

Sister-in-Law,

I can't reschedule. That's the only date I'm available.

Nothing will happen. Rallies take place all the time. Our jobs have become much easier thanks to the elephant. The whole square grows quiet whenever Amitabh makes an appearance. It's uncanny. Everybody stares at him, mesmerized.

I was walking him around the square on Wednesday when a few monks approached, staring at him, before they suddenly pressed their hands together and threw themselves on the ground. I was taken aback, but Amitabh stood still and observed the scene, as if people prostrating themselves before him was perfectly normal. Passersby stopped to watch as Amitabh took several leisurely steps and stretched out his trunk toward the flowers planted along the path.

How fragrant!

That's what he seemed to say. He breathed in a trunkful of the scent, then plucked a blossom which he tossed toward the monks. I was astonished. I imagine everybody else was too.

You get the picture. Amitabh's arrival defuses tensions in the square. And if you think about it, anti-war protestors in military formations make no sense. So, now the general consensus here seems to be that staging nonviolent protests is better.

But you know what, people at the company aren't too happy. They've spent a fortune acquiring the elephant. I reckon carrying him up to Level 321 alone would have cost an arm and a leg. If you also take into account the fuss they made over floor reinforcements, their initial investment must've been substantial. But far from helping with clashes, the elephant they spent so much on is preventing fights from happening altogether, so I expect the company is worried about losing all their business with the Beanstalk Security Guardhouse.

My bosses are determined to get the most bang for their buck. They want to use Amitabh as a tactical weapon as was originally planned, but he is such a softie. What kind of elephant makes no noise when he's walking! He tiptoes along with such dainty steps. Since we upped the ante and brought in an elephant, the protestors should have responded by at least throwing Molotov cocktails for my company to win more business, but there isn't a single child or adult in Beanstalk that hates Amitabh.

My point is that nothing will happen that day. It should be fine to meet on the scheduled date. You could come earlier to watch. I've mentioned several times that crowds of people show up just for the elephant, right? Yesterday was the same. The mood at the square was very strange, with people falling on their knees again and again before Amitabh. I feel like the leader of a cult or something.

Oh, there really are only a few days left. I'll see you soon.

Brother-in-law,

We waited for a long time but didn't get to see you in the end. We couldn't stay until the appointed time, but we did wait for ages in that ruckus.

My sister says it doesn't matter. According to her, she didn't go to Beanstalk to see you but to vacation there. We enjoyed ourselves for three days, though we splurged big time.

Prices were insanely high. I had assumed my sister would pay for everything but perhaps it got too expensive, seeing as I had to chip in a fair amount. But the resort on Level 410 was great. It had incredible views from the pool. Beanstalkians with sunburns are the wealthy ones, right? Everyone I'd seen while walking around in the lower levels was pale from always being indoors, but many at the pool were tanned.

As for my sister, she seems a little disappointed to have missed you, though she doesn't let on. While she eats well and goes about her business, I can tell she's secretly crestfallen.

At any rate, that day was an absolute fiasco. The sheer number of people gathered in that puny lot. We knew we had picked the wrong date the moment we stepped into the square, but we couldn't move the meeting place as we had no way to contact you, for heaven's sake. We'd arrived a bit early, given your enthusiastic promotion of the elephant. We wanted to see what the hype was about.

We did get to the meeting place but as you know, there were about five thousand protestors that day, packed all the way up to the fountain. Some four hundred were in front of the fountain alone. So you can imagine our reluctance to stand there.

"Hey. If we stand back here, will that dolt be able to notice us?" My sister actually asked me that absurd question.

"Obviously. What kind of man wouldn't recognize his wife?"

"If he sees us, he will. But my question is will he see us in this crowd."

It was a strange feeling, standing in the heart of a protest on foreign soil when I'd never been to one of this scale in my own country. I felt like I should join the chanting. We debated moving to another location but decided to stay, as it would be a hassle to go somewhere else then come back.

"We demand a peace treaty!
"Start talks with Cosmomafia!
"Stop bombing civilians!"

I shouted a few lines, but they didn't have rhythm. The protestors didn't seem too organized either. The protest wasn't at all like you described. I'm not sure it was peaceful—if anything, it felt as though a conflict could break out any minute.

Perhaps we had waited for thirty minutes. The path leading to City Hall was blocked by what looked like shipping containers; my first thought was that there must be construction going on, but soon I saw a horde of security guards rushing out from them. They held up their shields and formed tight rows—that's a phalanx, right? The mood darkened quickly and I didn't feel comfortable sticking around much longer. I suggested to my sister that we turn back, but she said we couldn't leave so soon after having made the trip there and should wait a bit more.

After another thirty minutes or so, we spotted you. Did you see us? We saw you from afar. People were saying, "Here comes Amitabul." They were referring to Amitabh as Amitabul, the Buddha of Infinite Light, right? They kept saying, "Hail Amitabul. Hail Amitabul." They seriously said that. They weren't actually praying but jokingly joined their palms together as they chanted "Hail Amitabul" like it were some celebrity's name, which after a while really did start to sound like a Buddhist mantra.

I'll admit it was a cool sight: when the elephant appeared at the square, security guards and protestors alike suddenly forgot what they were doing and stared at him, transfixed. To be honest I suspect they would've reacted the same way to any other bizarre spectacle. Anything everybody could stare at, not just an elephant, would have done the trick.

That didn't last long though. The mood quickly grew aggressive again. I heard people say things like, "Let's finish them today!" along with some very hostile words. I don't know if that day was especially bad, but I'd had enough. My sister agreed. We left when we saw the security guards swarming into the square soon after. Something was bound to happen then.

We did what we could, so don't blame us for not showing up at the appointed time Our decision was the right one, I believe. I was shocked when I read the paper later. I imagine you wouldn't have had the chance to come find us in that commotion anyway.

I'm sure there will be another opportunity to meet. Although it looks like we won't get to go to Beanstalk for some time because we practically blew all our money.

And I'm very sorry about the elephant. I hope you're not too devastated.

Sister-in-law,

Ah, you were waiting. I'm glad you two got out safely.

I had no idea there would be such a huge crowd that day.

I'm guessing five thousand protestors here in Beanstalk is tantamount to forty thousand in our country? The Security Guardhouse was put on alert when news came of protestors flooding into City Hall Square. All of the security guards were deployed, of course, and every single security company was ordered to mobilize too. I was on standby all afternoon and couldn't contact you in time. I thought you two wouldn't be foolish enough to stay put—you did well to leave.

Amitabh was unusually stressed that day. He wasn't sick or anything, but I could tell from the way he moved he was quite annoyed. Probably because my bosses kept putting him through charging practice. Claiming that we needed to showcase what other security companies couldn't, especially in these turbulent times, they were eager to send Amitabh into the protests, but the fact was he wasn't ready yet. Maybe he never would be. It wasn't in his nature to attack or frighten anyone.

He was a harmless elephant. There was nothing to worry about even when children passed right in front of him. Everybody knew that. No one was scared when he poked children with his trunk. Wait, I remember one exception. Amitabh wiggled his trunk at some dog that was hanging around him once, but then people who looked like bodyguards jumped out of nowhere and surrounded us—I was so shocked. And even then, Amitabh seemed to be more startled than the dog was. And they wanted me to train him to charge?

He'd been scolded the day before because he was making so little progress. Not that scolding solved anything. I'd never seen him run, let alone charge. War elephants had to trumpet a bit and stamp their feet menacingly on the ground, but he just shuffled his way *around* people. He was hopeless.

"You running a circus or what?"

That was the Tactical Research Director's daily refrain. He believed in weaponizing elephants. He's the one who told me they were weapons once upon a time too. That an approaching front-line army of elephants used to inspire terror in people who had never seen such creatures before, causing them to mistake the elephants for mythical monsters or demons incarnate from hell. This was two millennia ago. Using elephants against a close order formation, he says, isn't actually a very good tactic save for the intimidation factor. Controlling elephants is easier said than done and they panic easily when placed in battle. If a spear comes flying their way, they might turn around and crush the close order formation of their own troops. That's why my bosses kept insisting on training Amitabh for charges; they figured that since Amitabh was unusually calm by nature, he would make a pretty useful weapon if only he could be made to heed orders.

But in my mind, he was no weapon. He was a saint. Sometimes he really seemed like a Buddha. He loved the sound of "Amitabul," you know? Maybe because he knew it referred to him, but whenever we heard a chorus of "Amitabul, Amitabul" by the gathering crowd during our walks, he would flap his ears and survey everyone with a happy look on his face. No wonder people kept saying Amitabh was their new religion, repeating their mantras of "Hail Amitabul."

That Amitabh could charge was thus still unthinkable when the situation at the square was declared an emergency, and yet my bosses remained adamant about sending Amitabh in. I had to coax a very reluctant Amitabh down the flower path into the square, but from the moment we entered, I saw that the square was so jam-packed it would be impossible to take another step forward.

The sight must've overwhelmed Amitabh because he grew fidgety. Maybe he was nauseous. He whimpered a little, though the murmurs of "Hail Amitabul" seemed to gradually calm him. You heard it too, right? The babble of voices converging into a single hum at one point. "Hail Amitabul, Hail Amitabul." I was used to hearing the phrase but never from so many people. The chants from the multitude sounded like echoes filling the entire space. With each iteration, the echoes seemed to synchronize. I knew people were only chanting in jest, but by then I felt as though I were listening to a genuine mantra.

You know how cicadas sound like that too? They chirp individually but a melody and a rhythm emerge over time, as if the whole forest is singing. Amitabh heard his name ringing across the whole square and seemed to collect himself. His flapping ears stilled. Something had occurred to him. What could it be? Then I thought, a realization. The fella could've been having an epiphany that instant.

If you think about it, his life had been quite pitiful—an elephant that aimlessly roamed the lands of India alongside monks, fasting even, until waking up one day suspended from a tower crane, suffering the indignity of flailing his four legs in midair; the next day, strolling along a crimson flower path in a tiny square; then on still another day, being besieged by a square full of people and their "Hail Amitabul, Hail Amitabul." After all that, isn't it only fitting that he realizes *something*?

Then, I knew. Aha, something was imminent. I slid down the elephant's back and stood quietly next to him. I studied his face, which I felt definitely looked different. I wasn't the only one to think so. A hush fell around us. I looked up to see everyone in the vicinity gaze rapturously at Amitabh.

It was a curious feeling. Indescribable. I was witnessing up close the moment of enlightenment. How can I put that into words? How can I translate into language the moment when the elephant in my care was about to become a Buddha? And how could I know what was happening? I wasn't the enlightened one, Amitabh was. How had that truth been communicated to me?

I'd half-expected this moment to arrive someday, but not so abruptly without any warning. Having had no time to prepare myself, I was at a complete loss as to what I should feel or what I should observe.

So, I looked into his eyes. I couldn't tell what they were seeing, but they were clearly seeing something. What was it? Something outside of this world, or something inside himself?

Time froze. I knew that when this moment passed, this one moment, my friend would have finally broken the chain of suffering and become a Buddha. Oh, the great savior Buddha was arriving amid this chaos.

Then, the moment passed. Or rather, a split-second before that moment was able to pass, I heard a sound: *crack*!

Startled, I wheeled around and saw the Tactical Research Director from my company whip Amitabh's back with a long stick used during training, shrieking, "To your positions! Prepare for battle!"

At those words, Amitabh took a step forward. A step. Alas, just when he was about to become a Buddha, he had to come to his senses (or rather lost them) and walked off to his battle position. I was unnerved. I looked around and the spine-tingling moment from seconds before was gone without a trace. Though I was sure that a five-meter radius surrounding Amitabh had been feverishly hot, not a single piece of that tantalizing moment remained. Now, no one was looking at Amitabh. As though no one had been in the first place.

Had it been an illusion?

Amitabh was acting normally, just like everyone else. He'd gone back to being a gentle-to-a-fault elephant terrified of crowds, as if nothing had happened. It had to have been an illusion. I snorted with laughter. What on earth had I been thinking? An enlightened elephant? What gibberish. Buddha, my ass!

Amitabh seemed stressed. I led him along the flower path to his battle position, where the rest of the mounted guards were assembled. As animals easily get upset in crowded places, a large open space is required right behind the rest of the security guards so that they have a place to retreat to when tired. But even that space had little breathing room that day. Scores of personnel had been mobilized given the size of the protest. The space looked like a packed warehouse. I took Amitabh aside to where all the equipment was kept and tried to soothe him, but it was clear he wasn't ready for a charge.

Meanwhile, the situation at the square looked serious. You saw for yourself, right? With the protestors also forming a phalanx, the two sides stood face to face in that tiny area. Despite my bosses badgering us to deploy the elephant, we simply couldn't. Amitabh was already losing it, and the loud, distressing noises ricocheting around the square seemed to agitate him further—he began to swing his trunk left and right, too antsy to stand still. I was worried he'd snap.

I had to do something for him. That was the only thought in my mind. I saw a water tank nearby. It must've been for using in the water cannons during protest control—an alternative to using ceiling sprinklers, which is banned by fire safety regulations. It occurred to me that some water might do him some good. I opened the tank's drain valve, filled a bucket with water, and took it to Amitabh. When I held it right beneath his trunk, he finally seemed to perk up. He put his trunk into the bucket and sucked up the water. Heartily. Boy could he drink a lot. But the next moment, he started going berserk.

I was stunned. Amitabh suddenly lunged toward the phalanx of security guards. He reared up, spraying water from his trunk, shrieking in pain. I had never seen such a scene. Amitabh, the sweet elephant, launching himself at people. At security guards, no less.

The security guards looked back in alarm, and within seconds they had broken formation and were scrambling out of the way. Who could blame them? Survival before training. The phalanx had been breached. The protestors seized the opportunity to strike, by which point our phalanx was useless. Entire ranks of security guards collapsed, just like that.

Bewildered, I dipped a finger inside the bucket and tasted the water. Shit. It stung! Someone had mixed tear gas into the tank set aside for water cannons. What elephant wouldn't go berserk after sucking up a bucketful of that stuff? It would've been kinder to suspend him from a crane outside the building.

Amitabh went on a crazed rampage. Of course, he didn't give the protestors special treatment. He wasn't himself. He bolted after the protestors with sudden ferocity, scattering half of them in a flash. That gave him a clear view of a wide passage behind where the protestors had been standing, one that led to the south window.

Amitabh lurched toward it, parting protestors like the Red Sea and opening a wide path across the middle of the square. *Thump, galumph, thump, galumph.* It was a true charge. The charge that my bosses had so desperately wished for.

I dashed after him. The ground resounded and the cobblestones shattered but Amitabh didn't seem to want to stop. Shit, I felt so bad for him. I wanted to go comfort him somehow. He was such a good elephant, a true Buddha to Beanstalkians, yet he was suffering so much because of me.

The passage stretched on without a single obstacle. No one, of course, stood in the way. Amitabh ran and ran and ran. I did too. How long we ran, I don't know. A window came into view. It reflected the corridor perfectly like a mirror—two elephants hurtling towards each other, each with a man in hot pursuit.

"No!" I yelled but it was too late. What was probably fortified glass made to resist most kinds of impact stood no chance against Amitabh.

Instead of a thud, there was a crack, a crunch, something along those lines. The sound of being broken and pierced. Leaving that sound behind him, Amitabh escaped Beanstalk. Without a rope, without a tower crane, an untranquilized elephant shot out of a window on Level 321, flailing his four legs. Oh, Amitabh. Oh, Hail Amitabul.

"Hail Amitabul, Hail Amitabul." The protestors chanted Amitabh's name as they tore past the barricade of shipping containers and stormed City Hall. Their victory was decisive. But what good was that? The mayor was on the other side of the planet, as he always was whenever a crisis arose in Beanstalk. Presumably for an official overseas trip. Even though the protestor's victory was tactically a crushing one, it meant little strategically. There was little the protestors could gain from this fight.

Anyway, that's what happened. I was so busy sorting out the aftermath that I couldn't keep our appointment that day. I did go to our meeting point later on but I didn't see anyone.

I was gazing at the deserted fountain when I had the thought: he could've become a Buddha. Amitabh had definitely been on the verge of enlightenment. That moment flashed through my mind—that spine-tingling moment which I thought had vanished cleanly and tracelessly re-emerged, clear as ever. It hadn't been an illusion. It'd been real. Amitabh had truly been about to break the karmic cycle and reach nirvana.

At the time, why did I think I was hallucinating? If only I'd protected Amitabh at all costs, he would've gone on to become a living Buddha. I had ruined everything. Poor Amitabh.

Oh, why am I so pathetic?

Brother-in-law,

I can't believe I missed that moment of enlightenment! But perhaps it's best that I did.

My sister says the elephant would've gained enlightenment the moment he smashed the window, when he realized there was no floor to support his weight. But does enlightenment make you immune to pain? Wouldn't it still hurt, falling from Level 321? Whether he was enlightened or not would have made no difference then. It's not like reaching nirvana suddenly transports you to someplace else. What does it matter if he was or wasn't enlightened?

I obviously think the idea of an enlightened elephant is ludicrous. It sounds just about as plausible to me as a vegetarian dog. Not that I think you or my sister are ludicrous.

At any rate, now I understand why Beanstalk is reeling in shock. Does nobody know yet that you caused the incident? I'm concerned that you'll be held responsible one way or another as you were in charge of the elephant.

So, Brother-in-law, might I suggest you return home? Please do. I really don't think someone like you fits in at a place like that. Don't make us go find you again, just come back. My sister is waiting for you. I'm sure she won't welcome you with a shower of praises, but there still is a place for you here. Give it some thought.

Fully-Compliant

Grade Two Administrative Officer Choi Sinhak of the Intelligence Bureau stared at the person who had just asked him a question.

"Are you asking me because you really don't know?" Choi Sinhak said incredulously.

Feigning a look of absolute cluelessness, Councilor Go snapped, "Why would you expect me to know?"

Sitting up straight, Choi Sinhak explained once again why Cosmomafia was aiming an ICBM, an intercontinental ballistic missile, at Beanstalk. Councilor Go and the other councilors on the National Defense Committee sat listening, looking perfectly content with their roles of passive listeners.

What's with their expressions? They look like they're hearing this for the first time.

Though Choi Sinhak's explanation had been complicated and roundabout, the reason Beanstalk was being attacked was simple: Beanstalk attacked Cosmomafia first. Nobody had bothered doing an official count, but Beanstalk's raids on suspected Cosmomafia hideouts throughout the decade had caused at least 20,000 civilian casualties and displaced 800,000 refugees—more people than Beanstalk's total population.

Many of the general public were not aware of that fact. Not due to censorship but due to simple apathy. Therefore, the city government did not have to put out patently false information, though it did on occasion release slightly counterfactual statements which anyone with some sense could see through. Of course, councilors on the National Defense Committee were never given false information; defense was not to be trifled with. The councilors knew full well the gravity of the situation.

"Long story short, we're the ones that provoked this war," said Choi Sinhak.

"Excuse me," said Councilor Go, "how can a government representative say such a thing at a National Defense Committee meeting? That we *provoked* the war."

Beanstalk had deployed two aircraft carriers and conducted a series of bombings for twenty days and twenty nights. Ten days after the bombings began, the field commander reported that there were no targets left to attack, but Beanstalk did not withdraw the order to attack. The order that reached the battlefield was to continue the operation until decisive victory was achieved. Once they ran out of houses to destroy, the Navy's fighter-bombers dropped expensive precision-guided bombs on dilapidated tents and narrow mountain paths as though they meant to bomb all civilization in the area back to the Stone Age.

"Who on earth gave the order to wipe out the entire area?" asked Councilor Go.

Choi Sinhak swallowed. "Are you really sure you don't know who?" He was frustrated out of his mind. Five days ago, the Beanstalk Navy lost two of its three aircraft carriers. The damage would take more than two years to repair.

"Administrative Officer Choi. Who gave the final command?" Councilor Go pressed again.

Choi Sinhak could not reply, but it was not because he didn't know the answer. The City Council, to which the National Defense Committee belonged, was obviously the supreme command of the Beanstalk military. But the Council had not passed a formal declaration of war as Cosmomafia was not a nation, nor had it dispatched new troops to the area it meant to bomb as Beanstalkian forces had a standing base there. Although the Council had never officially approved the bombing mission, Choi Sinhak was sure there would have been a general consensus by political circles to mount the operation, behind which the interests of satellite-related corporations were no doubt involved.

And yet, as soon as the two aircraft carriers were lost, the Council was passing the buck and asking Choi Sinhak questions like, "Why was the order issued? Answer the question please."

"You're asking me why?" Words failed Choi Sinhak, countless thoughts flitting through his head. Among them was the thought that Beanstalk would finally bite the dust this time because the people in charge of keeping Beanstalk safe had questions to answer but were currently trying to hide behind questions of their own. This was the day when those responsible decided to shirk responsibility. And so Judgment Day approached.

"Is there any chance of Cosmomafia owning nuclear warheads?" asked Councilor Go.

"Very little," replied Choi Sinhak. *But it doesn't take a nuclear warhead to destroy a building,* he thought. "And Cosmomafia's precision guidance technology for ground targets isn't reliable. They aren't capable of hitting Beanstalk dead center from halfway across the world yet. That said …"

Choi Sinhak knew it was only a matter of time. Cosmomafia already had the technology to shoot down a satellite orbiting at the speed of Mach 3. Just because Judgment Day wasn't sweeping down on Beanstalk right this minute did not mean it was safe. What stood between Beanstalk and Doomsday was not an impregnable technological barrier but the mere practicality of repurposing an anti-satellite weapon to strike ground targets.

Councilor Go asked, "How long until they can hit ground targets?"

"Two years max," Choi Sinhak replied.

Instantly, peace descended upon the meeting room. A precarious peace thanks to an administrative technicality.

One that would last a maximum of two years, a minimum of six months.

What should I make of this calm? Do they think two years is a long time? They won't need to address the issue before their term in office ends, is that it? Are they not going to do anything then, again?

At any rate, peace seemingly settled over Beanstalk. But the councilors were not altogether idle. After the National Defense Committee meeting, money began to trickle out of Beanstalk, and for the first time in seventeen years, real estate prices showed signs of dropping, starting in the affluent districts on the highest floors.

"Folks sure move fast," said Choi Sinhak to an acquaintance. "Properties are pouring onto the market, so why's it taking so long for housing prices to crash?"

"Because there's a ton of buyers."

"Who? Are there any investors left when all the capital's moving abroad?"

"It seems like there's still enough domestic capital. Individual buyers."

"Individual buyers?"

"Yeah, people are buying those properties to actually live there."

The irony of the situation struck Choi Sinhak speechless.

Approximately two weeks after that conversation, Choi Sinhak's mother informed him over the phone that she had purchased a house with an indoor garden on Level 610. He cried out, "Why would you move there *now*? You should've asked me first."

"Shush. I've no wish to depend on my children nor let them tell me what to do. The price'll drop further, I hear, but by then the house might get sold so I snatched it up. So what if I lose some money? I don't have high expectations. There's a garden, too, how lovely is that? Oh, my heart. To think I had to send the little mutt away because we had nowhere to keep him. All my life I've dreamed of living in a house like that. Isn't it great? Don't worry about the money. I'm capable of paying that much."

That last sentence meant she had spent her entire fortune. His mother had always lamented having to give away their dog five years ago. So had Choi Sinhak. If only there had been space for him. The dog was smart. Befitting a dog born and bred in Beanstalk, he had excellent perception of three-dimensional spaces. Wherever you lost him, the clever creature found his way home by hitchhiking on elevators. Choi Sinhak had not given his cleverness much thought until one day after they gave him away, the dog reappeared as a celebrity. A film actor, no less. He had been cast in the lead role of a famous movie franchise about a canine drug investigator. Choi Sinhak had felt defeated when he heard that the pooch's house was more expensive than his. Damn.

"That's great, mother." Choi Sinhak could say no more.

The government was pulling out all the stops to attract foreign investors in an attempt to keep the capital market from crashing. One measure intended to entice Islamic financing through a bill waiving double stamp duty charges on real estate transactions that use a murabaha or ijarah structure.

When he heard about the government's efforts, Choi Sinhak blustered, "They passed what bill? Unbelievable. Beanstalk doesn't even have that many Muslims—is the government trying to milk every last bit of their money to fund moving costs for the filthy rich or what?"

He hated people who pretended to be patriots when everything was fine but would be the first to flee in times of real trouble. They did not truly love Beanstalk. He, Choi Sin-hak, did. He had absolute proof of his love for Beanstalk: his terraphobia.

He was only eleven when the Great Explosion on Level 520 happened. Emergency Evacuation Plan No. 1 took effect and while everyone young and old wormed their way out of the country, he did not leave. He could not leave. He had never before or since ventured anywhere below Level 50. At the time, he was scared but he had no choice. Descending to the ground floor was more terrifying to him than Beanstalk collapsing.

Of course, his condition was inconvenient in many ways. Imagine, an Intelligence Bureau agent incapable of overseas missions. But he did not consider his terraphobia an illness. He never even attempted to treat it. To him, it was a blessing. The task of protecting Beanstalk was his divine calling. That was why he couldn't help but despise those who tried to leave Beanstalk.

"Beanstalk doesn't even have that many Muslims."

Beanstalk in fact had about 2,700 Muslim residents, and Şehriban was one of them. This was her seventh year in Beanstalk already. She was getting used to life in Beanstalk now, but her first year had been constant tension. Since she was on an undercover infiltration mission, she never knew what might happen, nor when and where she would be given what order. More frightening was not knowing if she might be exposed. But with each passing day and change in season, her anxieties melted away. Such was the power of time.

Why aren't I getting any orders?

Şehriban grew older, her temporary interpreting job turning into a career she had pursued for over three years. The days were peaceful. Nothing happened. The Beanstalk Intelligence Bureau was laxer than she had thought, so much so that she probably wouldn't get caught even if she were to leave proof of her being a spy everywhere she went. The fight trickled out of her, the senses dulled. She had no occasion to raise a weapon. More than once she had doubts about Cosmomafia, which had left her on her own without contacting her once in years.

Her sixth year in Beanstalk marked a change in Şehriban's life. As her reputation as a professional interpreter grew, her income jumped. She started collecting handbags, initially out of a professional need. She had reluctantly purchased a small handbag so as not to feel outclassed by her clients, but over time, her wardrobe began to house too many bags for them to have been bought purely as a work requirement.

But Şehriban's expensive hobby of collecting bags was unsustainable. Her income was irregular. Sometimes she would have an overwhelmingly full schedule, while other times she would go weeks without work. If she didn't push herself during the busy season to take on more projects, she would have a harder time holding onto her clients during the quieter season. But Şehriban did not know that. So, when the Beanstalk economy started to take a hit from the falling property prices, clients dropped away until her dwindling income became cause for great concern.

I have no savings, but I feel iffy about selling off my handbags when I won't get a fair price for them.

She was also bored. She had not infiltrated Beanstalk for a life like this. Oh, what on earth was she doing? She let out a long sigh, meditating on the days gone by. Her family, her friends, the unsung souls who met painful deaths, her comrades. Overtime, her bloodstained rage had eroded like a tombstone in a desert; her burning courage lost its target and drifted like a misfired arrow. The days were embarrassingly uneventful. She wished she had not taken the oath. If only she had known it would lead to this.

Then one day, Şehriban was given an order at last. A Great Commission that spoke directly to her soul, impossible to defy: *You can't miss this! The Beanstalk ICBM Special Edition!*

Aah, a special edition! The chic zipper design symbolizing a ballistic missile flying toward Beanstalk, the large tree-shaped silver charm that was undeniably reminiscent of a mushroom cloud, the romantic red with an urban sensibility that oozes apocalyptic melancholy, the gentle yet bold leather handle that would wrap tenderly around her slender arm to the end of the world, and in a limited edition of only ten handbags to boot. This was no doubt a monumental bag she could not miss out on.

Desperate as she was for the bag, Şehriban did not have the money. For the first time in her life, she felt a compelling need to "touch base" with her clients. It was time to send them her regards. *Don't forget me!* She fished out the business cards that she had chucked carelessly into her bags. Smoothing their creases, she laid the cards out on the floor and called each of her clients, starting with the biggest ones.

I can't believe I'm doing this.

The very next day, another order was communicated to Şehriban via a newspaper headline: DOUBLE STAMP DUTY RELIEVED ON MURABAHA AND IJARAH TRANSACTIONS. A thrill ran through her body. The stage was now set for her to begin her mission for Cosmomafia. She was shortly given the order to proceed by her Cosmomafia contact.

It's finally time. After seven years.

He did not receive detailed instructions given the sensitive nature of his work, but Choi Sinhak knew what he had to do. The government was planning to relocate thirty-seven major agencies down 150 levels or so. In other words, Beanstalk's entire seat of government had to be moved down as much. The government also intended to install at least three layers of shock absorbers on the upper floors in preparation for a missile attack.

"We are fully capable of intercepting the missiles" was the official statement put out by the government, but it was not the truth—Beanstalk was in fact preparing to absorb any incoming missiles with the body of the building, but this was a secret of course. There was no guarantee the building would remain intact. That was also a secret.

Choi Sinhak's mission was to sell state-owned properties in the upper levels and acquire new locations for the government in the lower levels. Trading real estate was clearly a de-motion from intelligence work, but the gravity of the mission suggested a promotion. The "sell high, buy low" rule applied here, but to do that Choi Sinhak had to act fast before any rumors rocked the real estate market. He formed a team of Beanstalk's top real estate experts, which was expensive, but money was not a concern. The work was not as challenging as he had expected, and in fact the bulk of it was done by skilled professionals from the private sector including major financial institutions and law firms, which allowed him to simply focus on his role as team leader.

Choi Sinhak stressed to his team, "Information must be kept strictly confidential."

"Of course. You have nothing to worry about," his colleagues replied.

Half a year passed in that manner. Before Choi Sinhak's team began buying up properties in earnest, however, the real estate prices from Levels 150 to 200 began to rise. Choi Sinhak checked the real estate transactions conducted in the area and most of them, it turned out, were by political insiders. He swore. He had half-expected this, of course. As the acquisition costs for the new seat of government were going appallingly over budget, he might even have to redo the plan from scratch after having worked on it for six months.

But something else bothered Choi Sinhak while he went through the data. Several foreign banks had also begun purchasing certain properties between Levels 150 and 200 for higher-than-market prices, which appeared to be driving up selling prices in the whole region.

"They shouldn't buy stuff up like that. Since when were

banks allowed to buy real estate anyway?" asked Choi Sinhak.

"Banks? That's impossible," replied a colleague. "Let's see … ah, they're banks in Southeast Asia. They're probably just providing Islamic financing to clients. I bet they're doing ijarah transactions. Or diminishing musharakah structures. The double stamp duty issue has been resolved, but financial regulators haven't decided what type of transaction ijarah is. So …"

Choi Sinhak nodded while privately thinking, *What does any of that mean?*

In any case, money was coming in from unexpected sources, thanks to which real estate prices remained relatively stable, allowing the fleeing rich to move their assets overseas and get rid of their properties at full price. The pricks who would gladly be ground dwellers on foreign soil as long as they got to keep their money.

He remembered what his mother had said a few days earlier: "Surely, a missile wouldn't hit us? That would never happen, right?"

"Right," he had replied.

"There we go. It's just the madcaps emigrating, mind you. The rest of us aren't so fussy. I heard if a missile comes flying at us, we can shoot it down. Can't be sucked in by wild rumors when my son's an Intelligence Bureau agent, can I now?"

What his mother did not know was that Beanstalk's chances of successfully shooting down a missile was less than thirty percent. Neither did most of its citizens. If that day really arrived, the city could minimize casualties by issuing an emergency evacuation order, but it could do nothing about damages to property. No insurance company covered property damage arising from war. Yet Choi Sinhak withheld that information from his mother—no, he withheld it from everyone. He did not sell his own property either. Quite a few insiders had already started to, but not him.

Choi Sinhak's role was not to handle real estate transactions directly, it was simply to put together a team and diligently collect information. But the more he mobilized his intelligence network, the more suspicious he grew of one particular detail.

"Aren't those foreign banks acting a little odd? Why do they keep raising real estate prices? Disrupting the market like that wouldn't work in their favor at all."

The influx of Islamic capital, especially from Southeast Asia, was not of course completely detrimental to all of Beanstalk. As funds were slipping out of the real estate market in the Level 500s and 600s, the injection of Islamic and other foreign capital was playing a major role in preventing that market from crashing. The arrival of institutional investors backed by oil money was welcome news to the city government, not least because the Level 500s and 600s were home to many massive properties that individual buyers could not afford.

But the Level 150s, in which nobody had previously been interested, was a different story. The banks were plainly acquiring properties for unreasonably high prices. Rumors that they had caught wind of city-backed redevelopment plans were already going around in some circles. There was now mounting interest in the district from individual investors as well.

Are they doing it on purpose? What's their deal?

Even as she carried out her mission as ordered, Şehriban's thoughts occasionally turned to the ICBM Special Edition. The handbag had been out for a while but there still seemed to be stock left, perhaps due to its hefty price tag. Or maybe it was not a true limited edition. But no matter, it was, Şehriban felt, a handbag fated to be hers. She imagined a distant future: years later, while recounting to someone the mission she had undertaken in these times of chaos and tumult, how nice would it be if the bag was sitting on the table?

Suddenly aware that she had been smiling to herself, Şehriban snapped out of her daydream and looked up. The bank employee overseeing ijarah transactions was eyeing her quizzically. The evaluation must have ended. "Are we done already?" Şehriban asked.

"Yes. Everything's been processed," the employee answered.

It was easy. Too easy. She was amazed at how simple it was to buy a house with the bank's money. Of course, she had received help from Cosmomafia. Its assurances that it would take care of the finances and all Şehriban had to do was ensure the mission went smoothly was no idle boast. Even after seven years. Cosmomafia had not broken its promise.

Şehriban gained confidence once she cleared this first step of her mission. She was relieved that her plans, which had been months in the making, were actualizing without major hiccups. Then, a thought crossed her mind: if the bank was so ready to give her money with no strings attached, might *that* also be possible?

She phoned the store that had the ICBM Special Edition, "the last one left in stock." A few hours later, she went to the bank and signed a murabaha contract. The bank paid the seller then handed Şehriban the ICBM Special Edition, although the bank would technically retain ownership of it. Having agreed to buy it back from the bank in one year at seven percent higher than the original price, Şehriban finally got her hands on the bag of her dreams.

"Are we done already?" Şehriban found herself asking again. "This really worked even for a bag?"

"Yes. Everything's been processed."

She was essentially taking out a loan with a seven-percent interest rate to buy the bag. But on paper, no interest had been charged. The arrangement was necessary as Islamic law prohibits interest.

Thank God!

It was with delight that Şehriban continued on her mission. Her new ICBM Special Edition slung over her shoulder, stride elegant, she went around meeting with realtors. And as she had been instructed seven and a half years ago, she set out to purchase a total of seventeen properties. Five of them were scattered across the upper-level outskirts, while the rest were concentrated in the center of Levels 130 to 165.

It was not long before rumors circulated among the local realtors about a bigshot who was throwing around oil money. Added to that were comments about Şehriban's looks and soon the rumors evolved into bizarre tales. The rumor that she was protected by a powerful ally—a foreign government no less—began to spread, degenerating into a story so preposterous that it never reached Choi Sinhak's ears. Undetected by Choi Sinhak, Şehriban was able to secure eight of her seventeen targets in three months, all through Islamic financing.

Around the same time, Choi Sinhak was examining the purchase history of banks to puzzle out why Southeast Asian banks seemed so eager to raise real estate prices around Level 150. Then, he ran into something truly baffling: the "ICBM Special Edition." He had found records of a bank directly purchasing what only appeared to be a somewhat expensive bag.

An institution buying a single bag? What's going on?

Choi Sinhak summoned a real estate expert in his team who used to work at a law firm, and he proceeded to study Islamic finance in depth.

"I see. Then what's ijarah?" he asked the real estate expert.

"Ijarah is like a lease. The bank buys a house or a car or whatever the customer wants to buy on their behalf. The bank gives it to them and collects regular payments. The total amount repaid will obviously be bigger than the original cost of the purchase—bigger by the amount of interest. But the interest wouldn't exist anywhere on paper."

"That's the same thing as a long-term lease then," said Choi Sinhak.

"Not exactly," replied the colleague, "The ownership of the property passes to the bank."

"Why is that?"

"It's considered a sin to make money on money without trading tangible assets. So, the ownership of a tangible asset has to change hands. In this case, as with a murabaha, the ownership passes to a bank first. That's why banks whose main business is Islamic financing were less affected by the last financial crisis. Because they had tangible assets."

"So you're saying," said Choi Sinhak, "on paper the bank is buying, when really, the bank isn't buying …"

"The bank's giving a loan, pretty much," replied the colleague. "The bank *looks* like the buyer, but the real buyer's the customer who borrowed from the bank. Or a bond investor. Though of course, it wouldn't be called a bond in Islamic finance. Anyway, both steps of the transaction used to be taxed in Beanstalk—once when the ownership passes to the bank and again when it passes to the customer. What the Double Stamp Duty Relief Act does is view them as one transaction. They *are* the same transaction, really. But our financial regulators aren't clear on this point yet, so they've put down the bank as the bag's purchaser. They've viewed the bank as an investment company of sorts."

Choi Sinhak said, "That means whoever's raising real estate prices in the Level 150s might not be Southeast Asian institutional investors. It could be an individual."

"Right," confirmed the colleague.

"Uh, couldn't you have told me that sooner?"

"Uh, I believe I've explained this to you many times."

By the time Choi Sinhak finally caught up with her, Şehriban had already acquired her twelfth target. Choi Sinhak scrutinized her purchase history, and it could not have been fishier. Though Şehriban was quite a well-respected professional interpreter, she could not have become a real estate big shot with that job alone.

Does she really have a patron then …?

Choi Sinhak used his intelligence network to verify the rumors flying around, causing a fair amount of resistance from Beanstalkian agents stationed overseas. "You want me to investigate what? Do you have any idea how dangerous that is? Investigate the king's lovers? Wow."

Despite the number of complaints brought to him, in three days' time he was forwarded surprisingly detailed information. The subject was undoubtedly interesting, but the results were of course not so gripping: the rumors were all concluded to be false.

Choi Sinhak began to conduct site visits of properties Şehriban had bought, and he had only inspected three sites before he spotted a glaringly odd pattern. All three places had too long a history by Beanstalkian standards. They were not just old but as old as Beanstalk itself. Not once had they renovated the interior, nor changed their business.

"Why do you think she picked out these places to acquire?" Choi Sinhak wondered.

"I'm not sure," replied a colleague. "Maybe she wants to turn them into heritage sites."

"That wouldn't be bad in itself," said Choi Sinhak. "The property owners though—why would they put their properties up for sale now, when they haven't for decades?"

"Well they're getting paid a premium for it. As you know,

there could be a market meltdown any time, so they've made a reasonable choice on their part."

"Even if that's true, doesn't something still feel off?"

Choi Sinhak brooded. Why? Why had the banks authorized every murabaha or ijarah without any obvious collateral? Who was this woman? On the eve of doom, for what glory and riches was she throwing such an extravagant money party in Beanstalk?

Indeed, it did not hurt Beanstalk to have incoming capital, but that money was certainly not flowing in to make the country a better place. The money would stay while it made profit and then leave. Choi Sinhak believed Beanstalk was already under attack, an attack mounted by those who did not see Beanstalk as a place where people lived but simply as a real estate market. In fact, those on the frontline of the attack were not even outsiders; Beanstalkians who were supposed to be defending their homeland were doing the opposite.

Come to think of it, that's the kind of crap I've been doing too.

Choi Sinhak reminded himself of his mission. Home prices. He had to bring them under control. Then, it hit him. What if someone had learned of Beanstalk's plans to relocate the city's administrative center and was trying to raise the real estate prices in the new center around Level 150? But was there a reason to? Possibly. If Beanstalk managed to identify signs of a missile launch, it could issue an evacuation order one or two days in advance to avoid heavy casualties. It was highly unlikely that a Doomsday scenario would come to pass, but Beanstalk could not avoid damage to its facilities. The government had devised a relocation plan precisely for that reason. By its calculation, a missile attack would wreak nearly irreparable damage to Level 300 and above. That was why it had to move to the lower floors out of harm's way— move its property, that is, not its people.

If I were Cosmomafia, I'd try to trap the government at its current location before attempting an attack. Which means that woman is ...

He jumped to his feet. Why had he not seen it earlier? At last, he saw the big picture. It was Cosmomafia.

This was a very serious matter. The banks had been in on it. Not only that, the City Council had acted with them, seeing how it passed the Double Stamp Duty Relief Act at such an opportune moment. That might have been all the Cosmomafia sympathizers in the City Council were capable of, but it was enough.

It was enough for Şehriban at least. She had already gotten hold of the fourteenth location. Only three properties remained. Doomsday was now closer than ever.

The fourteenth property was the largest gym in Beanstalk. And like the other properties Şehriban bought, it had operated at the same spot since construction on Beanstalk was finished.

"This place isn't shariah-compliant," remarked Şehriban.

At which the gym owner replied, "You're right. The showers are separate, but the fitness facilities ..."

"I don't mean to blame you at all. None of us do. If anything, you've safeguarded this place well. Now that you've handed it over to us in such perfect condition, God will soon use it as He sees fit."

"God's peace be with you," said the gym owner.

"God's peace be with you. Please leave Beanstalk as soon as possible. On your way out, don't look behind you no matter what you hear. If you know what I mean," she joked.

Şehriban smiled as she stood up and mulled over the words, "God's peace." Was this the kind of peace God wanted? A peace achieved through bloody revenge could not possibly be the peace God wished to see. Though their country was a civilization splattered with blood, Beanstalkians as seen from inside Beanstalk were not the evil race she had thought them to be when she lived outside it. On the contrary, she might even describe most of them as kindhearted.

On her way back home, Şehriban was followed. She did not bother trying to shake off her tail, but escaping Beanstalk before Doomsday seemed highly unlikely now.

Şehriban's presentiment was not unfounded—Choi Sinhak had had travel restrictions placed on her. Then, directing all his energy to proving the link between Cosmomafia and the Islamic financiers, he found that the link between the two was not all that obvious. As Cosmomafia was reported to have been founded on Soviet military equipment and technology that had leaked out amid weakened controls after the USSR's collapse, it was utterly different in character from Islamic terrorist groups. Yet it was using Islamic finance?

Islamic finance was of course not exclusive to Muslims, no more than "green funds" were exclusive to environmental organizations. Muslims were free to use conventional finance just as non-Muslims were free to use Islamic finance. Anyone who wanted to follow God's will to prohibit interest could subscribe to Islamic finance as they would any other socially-conscious financial product. Granted, there would always be relatively more Muslim users.

To assure customers that their financial products complied with God's will, banks tasked a Shariah Committee made up of shariah scholars to verify the products. It was precisely this point that puzzled Choi Sinhak. The banks had to avoid investing in businesses related to alcohol, gambling, pork, or weapons, but here they were joining forces with Cosmomafia. How odd.

Choi Sinhak perused the intelligence reports on Cosmomafia's funding. There was something he could not quite grasp concerning its precision guidance technology for ground targets. While all signs pointed to Cosmomafia having started to develop the technology, it seemed to be struggling to fund the project. He could not rule out the possibility that it was receiving cash under the radar, but his conclusion was that it was woefully underfunded. That was why intelligence was hell-bent on finding and blocking Cosmomafia's mystery funding source. But Choi Sinhak considered another possibility: what if Cosmomafia had no intention of destroying Beanstalk with a missile? That immediately led to another question. If Cosmomafia had no intention of actually hitting Beanstalk with a missile, why was it dabbling in real estate? Was it hoping to get rich from property speculation? Indeed, it was well on its way to earning big money. But if there was no missile launch, the government wouldn't have to push ahead with the relocation, in which case real estate prices would fall back down.

Reviewing the list of fourteen properties Şehriban had purchased, Choi Sinhak grew certain that she was not out to simply raise the price of land. The properties had one very clear thing in common: they were the oldest establishments in Beanstalk. Places that had defended their spots for no less than sixty-five years without a single refurbishment, looking exactly like they had when they were first built.

He got someone to check if there were any other such properties that had not been sold yet. There were five more. Three of them were near the Level 150 region, which concerned the government's relocation plans.

First off, I'll have to acquire them.

It was time for Choi Sinhak to loosen the purse strings.

A few days later, Cosmomafia sent Beanstalk an ultimatum. It laid down no fewer than fourteen conditions, which the Beanstalkian government had no plans to accept. The government refused to even consider such threats as it was not dealing with a nation. Unofficially though, it could not afford to be so nonchalant. All available reconnaissance satellites were enlisted and analysts busily set to work. Though the might of its Navy had weakened considerably since Cosmomafia bombed two of its aircraft carriers, Beanstalk's intelligence capabilities were still intact. It could not send bombers to every suspicious location, but as long as it obtained exact coordinates of the missile launch site, it had at least a twenty-percent chance of mounting a successful preemptive attack. If only it could get precise coordinates.

Unfortunately, a thorough search yielded no traces of Cosmomafia's launch site. When claims came forth that missiles might not be the intended delivery system, the Beanstalk Emergency Security Meeting ordered stricter border inspections.

Funds leaked out of Beanstalk fast. The stock market deflated. The population trickled out. The neighboring country released a statement declaring that should Beanstalk activate Emergency Evacuation Plan No. 1 without consultation again, it would view the action as an invasion. That sent a flurry of people rushing out of Beanstalk before the situation grew even more serious.

Choi Sinhak aimed to buy a restaurant by paying a fifty-percent premium on the market price, but he immediately ran into an obstacle. The owner refused to sell. So did two other owners of similar properties. He made even higher offers to no avail. The following day, he received news that one of the restaurants had been sold for double the market price. The buyer was obviously Şehriban.

Although the links between Cosmomafia, Islamic financiers, and Şehriban had yet to be confirmed, Choi Sinhak was almost certain what was happening in Beanstalk.

A missile was flying in from the past—the bombs were already inside Beanstalk.

Choi Sinhak abandoned working on the government relocation, which now seemed pointless, and instead concentrated on buying the two remaining properties. He had to find evidence. To do that, he had to secure at least one of the remaining two places. Property prices leapt. Rumors were rife that the government was up to something, causing funds to pour into the neighborhood. The rumors included talk of the government planning to move down the capitol, which had been true, but was not anymore. Real estate prices had skyrocketed so much that acquiring land in the lower levels was practically out of the question unless the government intervened.

"Team Leader Choi. Why the hell aren't you buying?" asked the Secretary-General of the Emergency Security Meeting. "I don't think you understand your mission."

Choi Sinhak finally reported his findings about Şehriban. He also included an explanation about the government relocation being impossible, given the staggering amount of funds flooding into the new site from wealthy residential districts on the Level 500s and 600s.

"My old dog apparently moved there too," Choi Sinhak added. "That says it all."

"Huh? Anyway, you said there are bombs in here already. Do you have any evidence?" asked the Secretary-General.

"Not yet, but the circumstances point in that direction."

"You've got nothing?"

"I intend to obtain some evidence soon."

"How?"

"I'll need to get search warrants."

"If nothing turns up in the search, we'll all look like fools you know."

Choi Sinhak got his search warrants for the fifteen properties purchased by Şehriban. Then, he looked like a fool. There was nothing. Explosives aside, he detected nothing remotely resembling a bomb, not even a Jägerbomb—more than half of the restaurants he visited were halal and didn't serve liquor.

Choi Sinhak had failed spectacularly. A public outcry ensued, with accusations that the government was targeting halal restaurants based on unfounded conspiracy theories. Critiques abounded that Beanstalk was swerving toward insular nationalism, prompting "terraphobic nationalism," that age-old gripe against Beanstalk, to rear its ugly head. But Choi Sinhak was unperturbed—he was more preoccupied by the fact that he had found nothing and by the brief glimpse of Şehriban he had caught on one of the premises.

Maybe she's really just a speculator?

The date of attack Cosmomafia had announced was only a week away, but the missile launch site had still not been discovered. Choi Sinhak was not at all surprised. He was, however, disconcerted that the places he had suspected of containing a bomb had also turned up nothing.

Şehriban sat alone and went over the steps of assembling a bomb in her head. It had been so long since she last touched one that she could not be sure if what she remembered would work. Frankly, she was not convinced that the bombs would even explode. They had lain forgotten for decades in places where hands could not touch.

There were eight bombs in total. She had to connect each of them to a detonator, all of which were stored in different properties, then manually operate the devices the old-fashioned way to set the timer—it was not an easy task. Eight bombs, nine detonators. There was one extra detonator as one of the bombs was responsible for the Great Explosion on Level 520 which happened years back.

Şehriban would assemble the bombs in six days' time. Because they were such old models, they were enormous in order to obtain the kind of power capable of demolishing Beanstalk. If she removed them from their locations early, she would have no place to hide them.

She decided to abandon two bombs. The real estate prices of their storage places had shot up too high for even Şehriban to lay her hands on them.

I don't get this country. Why does a goddamn dog need real estate? How is he so rich anyway?

I don't get these people, thought Choi Sinhak. It was two days before the forewarned Judgement Day. Where were the bombs? They were definitely huge if they had been in Beanstalk since the time of its construction. Bombs hidden so long ago could not be small. Where were they planted? Inside the walls? Impossible. If you drilled through a wall, you would drill straight into the house next door. You could not drill into the floor either.

But ... hang on!

Choi Sinhak took out floorplans of the seventeen properties that Şehriban had bought and their surrounding areas. He could not find any empty spaces, but a floorplan hiding certain spaces was not unheard of. For one, the mayor's private elevator that ran from his office to the underground bunkers was perfectly invisible on the floorplan; the official map had been tinkered with. It was easy enough to erase an undeniably real space by drawing the surrounding space a little larger than it actually was.

Choi Sinhak dropped by the Intelligence Bureau the next morning, grabbed a few GPS receivers, and went down to Level 147. They were powerful location-tracking devices with millimeter-level accuracy. He arrived at a hospital, the fourth property Şehriban had purchased. He had no search warrant—this was no time for such formalities. Attaching the GPS receivers to various points on the hospital's outer walls, he read the location signals.

I knew it!

The locations did not match up. The hospital sat twelve more centimeters to the north than it did on the floorplan. The real walls had slightly smaller spans too. All the buildings nearby were the same, each slightly smaller than what had been mapped.

Judgment Day was imminent. With one day to go before the scheduled missile launch, Cosmomafia disclosed the locations of six launch sites simultaneously. Beanstalk was on the verge of issuing Emergency Evacuation Plan No. 1.

Şehriban put a sledgehammer in a golf bag, which she slung over her shoulder. She then went around smashing the walls of buildings she had bought and extracted the bombs. Hooking up the detonators to the bombs, she set the timer with her own hands. She broke out in a cold sweat. Would they even work properly? What if they suddenly exploded instead? Şehriban recalled the Great Explosion on Level 520.

One of the old bombs simply going off on its own accord was always a possibility.

Choi Sinhak visited the Emergency Security Meeting's Secretariat to obtain a warrant, but no one there took him very seriously. All of their attention was focused on whether they should issue Emergency Evacuation Plan No. 1. The members of the meeting were divided into two camps: "Absolutely do not proceed with the evacuation" versus "Proceed no matter what." There was no middle ground.

The question at hand was whether Cosmomafia was actually capable of hitting Beanstalk dead-on from thousands of kilometers away. While most of the meeting's participants were skeptical on this point, the proponents of evacuation believed it was necessary, even if Cosmomafia's chances of success stood at only ten percent. The opponents to evacuation argued that overreacting to every threat could cause Beanstalk's economy to implode even without a missile strike. Both sides had a point.

Yet the very discussion of an emergency evacuation plan struck Choi Sinhak as a sort of betrayal. Desert Beanstalk? It was unthinkable. At least the civil servants and the councilors—the mayor if nobody else—had to share their fate with Beanstalk to the final moment. But that was too much to ask of civilians. As soon as civilians crossed his mind, Choi Sinhak leaned towards executing the emergency evacuation plan. He knew of an existing threat, and he had proven half of his hypothesis. The other half would be easy enough to prove—he was confident about that. Except nobody was listening to him.

"So where's the evidence?" asked the Secretary-General of the Emergency Security Meeting.

"I can bring it to you in two hours," replied Choi Sinhak, "if you just give me a warrant."

"I already gave you one before. If you found nothing then, what makes you think you'll find anything now? Is the other side stupid? You should've found something the first time. Even if there once had been something, it'd be hidden by now."

"I just haven't found them yet, but the bombs are still there in the same spots."

"You can suddenly see what you couldn't before? With what?"

"With this," said Choi Sinhak as he held out a GPS receiver and the location measurement records. "The location on the floorplan was different from the actual location. The span of each wall's been shrunken a bit, as you can see, to hide a space. A space that can fit a pretty big explosive."

Choi Sinhak was sure he was right this time. But the Secretary-General still did not believe him. "Does this look like the moment for hide and seek to you? You think we have the time to play along with your games?"

"You think I'm playing games?" asked Choi Sinhak incredulously.

"There are six missiles. If just one of those hits the mark, we're goners."

"One search is all I need. I'm not telling you to ignore the missiles altogether."

"When was Cosmomafia founded? Not even fifteen years

ago. Beanstalk? Sixty-five years ago. How could they have buried bombs inside Beanstalk?"

"I told you, the bombs were brought in while Beanstalk was being built. Cosmomafia didn't bury them," said Choi Sinhak. "But whoever did, bombs are bombs."

"How would you prove the bombs were brought in back then? First you embarrass me in front of everyone," replied the Secretary-General, "and now you want me to get the same warrant for you again, in this state of affairs? Do you think I'm some vending machine for warrants? If you were to screw up again, it really wouldn't be funny this time."

Far from helping Choi Sinhak, the Secretariat locked him up.

After Şehriban finished setting up all eight bombs, she returned home and went to bed early. Her original plan of escape was no longer feasible. She couldn't sleep. Of course she couldn't. She had no regrets about the enormity of her actions. She simply waited for Emergency Evacuation Plan No. 1 to take effect. *Then I won't have to die.*

She lay staring numbly up at the ceiling, pointless thoughts filling her head. *Judgment Day, huh.* Could people judge people? Şehriban thought of her family and friends who had died in devastating succession before immediately erasing them from her mind. She did not need the victims to help her stick to her resolve. She had to be able to do this much without them. She had made her decision more than ten years ago after much deliberation. Some people had made their decisions sixty-five years ago, back when Beanstalk was being built. Watching Beanstalk add floor after floor, they had naturally associated it with the Tower of Babel. *Look how massive it is. It's got human vanity written all over it. It'll be another Babel.*

So, they planted bombs inside it. That would have been impossible to do once the building was complete but was very possible at the time—the construction site was a mess. Since the project was stupendously expensive, construction paused whenever it lost funding. So did the architectural design. The building work stopped and resumed twenty-three times, each time the design changing with it. Beanstalk was competing with another Tower of Babel being erected on the other side of the planet. The two towers revamped their designs endlessly to outbuild each other. They grew taller, wider. The race continued until one utterly defeated the other. Smuggling in a few bombs in the midst of that confusion was really not that hard.

The bombs had been carried in under divine names. They were like a prophecy, meant to be used when the time came by whoever needed them. No one knew who would use them, but there had been a conviction that someone would surely do so. Though no one would have expected it to take sixty-five years.

But had Beanstalk truly turned into a Tower of Babel? Şehriban rolled over to her side. She thought of the people who had lived here all these years, cradling a bomb. They must have had very high offers from some buyers, or faced unbearably brutal pressures. And yet they had stayed where they were for sixty-five years. They had kept the decades-old promise, many of them involving their own children in the cause. Hugging a bomb without knowing when it might explode. Şehriban had carefully observed their faces when they handed over their properties to her. Her own eyes had asked them, *Do you really think Beanstalk turned into a Tower of Babel?* They gave her no reply.

She could not sleep for the life of her. Should she disarm them? Those blasted bombs.

Despite being "locked up," Choi Sinhak was not monitored too closely. So, on the morning of Judgment Day, he was able to slip out of his confinement quarters, and after grabbing a few tools from home, dash to one of the restaurants containing a bomb. He was alone, with no backup. Ignoring the stares of passersby, he raised a heavy hammer and pummeled the full-height glass front of the restaurant. The fortified glass did not shatter as easily as he had hoped. The hammer kept bouncing back, ringing violently his hands.

I can't believe I'm doing this.

But he had to go through with it. If he succeeded in smashing the glass and breaking in, the alerted security guards would rush to the scene and at least inspect the premises to check for missing items. But before the security guards could even arrive, he felt a cold blade press against his neck.

"This is no way for a gentleman to behave, is it now?" said a voice from behind him. "Let us talk this out."

It was Cosmomafia. A murderous aura exuded from the assassin, who had a surprisingly kind face. He dragged Choi Sinhak to Şehriban's house and left him there, presumably to let her finish the job. Although, the assassin was a complete stranger to Şehriban as well. The realization that there had been a Cosmomafia assassin this whole time made her hair stand on end.

I guess he was sent to take me out? That knife would be on my throat if I didn't do my job properly or was caught beforehand.

Then, another thought hit her. *I thought I'd done this purely of my own free will, but even that wasn't true.*

Emergency Evacuation Plan No. 1 never came into effect. At the scheduled hour, Cosmomafia fired a few missiles. Tension rippled throughout the building as people waited, but none of the missiles came anywhere near. Peace was restored, even if it was to be short lived.

Şehriban blinked hard a few times, then said to Choi Sinhak, "You're from the Intelligence Bureau, right? You've figured it out, haven't you?"

Choi Sinhak nodded instead of answering.

Şehriban hung her head without a word. After a long moment, she asked, "Have I failed then?"

Choi Sinhak shook his head and said, "No. Nobody believed me."

"Does that mean …?"

"I couldn't disarm the bombs," said Choi Sinhak.

"I see. You couldn't disarm them either."

"Nope. Me neither."

God thus took back the brief reprieve granted Beanstalk. Then, He replaced it with silence. Judgment Day was still on.

Choi Sinhak did not question Şehriban on why she had done such a terrible thing. He did not want to. He was not so shameless as to not know why Beanstalk was being attacked. Şehriban was the same. She understood where he was coming from, and vice versa.

Choi Sinhak broke the extended silence. "How much time do we have left?"

Şehriban put up two fingers. "About two hours."

It was too late to turn things back. The clock continued to tick absently. Şehriban said, "Hey. If we're going to wait anyway, wouldn't it be better to go somewhere with a nice view. But this setup would remain the same—you know that, right? You're the prisoner, I'm the guard."

They went up to the public observatory on Level 670. Standing by the window and looking down, Choi Sinhak had zero desire to fight. Even if he managed to dodge out of Şehriban's sight, he had no way to stop the explosion. No one had believed him. Neither did he have a sudden desire to escape the building.

Choi Sinhak gazed down at the scene that stretched beneath the observatory. The ground was unfathomably far, and everything utterly quiet. He felt perfectly tranquil as he stared down in silence. This had to be the greatest blessing Beanstalk had ever offered him. At least from here, he was not terrified of looking squarely at the ground surface. At least from this height, he could take in the two-dimensional space lying below and not worry about retching.

What if Beanstalk had been taller—would he have felt even more serene then? Serene enough to not fear death? Choi Sinhak believed that the afterlife was two-dimensional. All terraphobes did. Buildings crashing and humanity falling toward a flat plane devoid of a vertical axis—that had been his idea of Doomsday. And that horrible moment was looming right before his eyes. He stared down. Just as people living on the ground would gape up at the sky at their final moment, he peered down at the ground with unfocused eyes. *Oh, drat.*

Şehriban lifted her eyes to the sky. She felt as if she were standing in the middle of the heavens. She was, in fact. *This was how God must feel.* Was that what made Beanstalk wicked? The fact its inhabitants knew how God felt? But what she felt now seemed harmless enough.

Soon, no one would be able to experience this feeling anymore. Standing still on steady ground, watching the world from God's vantage point. Such folly would be impossible for ages to come now. It was only feasible here.

A low cloud drifted closer and bumped into the glass wall. She could almost feel the moisture. The next moment, a wind blew, sweeping away the mist. The glass wall of the observatory quickly wiped away its tears and proudly faced the sky with dry eyes. Perhaps God's peace was *this* then—the immense heaven and earth visible through the dry window.

Şehriban looked beside her. Choi Sinhak was glued to the glass wall, eyes downcast. He did not seem at all frightened about looking down at the vast, dizzyingly distant earth from Level 670. Standing three steps back from the glass, Şehriban thought death would somehow feel much more concrete if she looked down. She was suddenly scared of dying. She thought she had made up her mind seven years ago, but the conclusion she had reached back then seemed no longer valid. It was natural that she should change her mind. She had lived seven more years since then. *Yes, what was wrong with Beanstalk? So what if it was a Tower of Babel?* She had not seriously considered this for a long time, but now that she did, she realized she did not necessarily hate Beanstalk.

Şehriban remembered her comrades who had perished in a bombing. At the time, she did not shed tears for them. She had come to Beanstalk with dry eyes, vowing to destroy it. Fervently wishing God's peace upon this land, Şehriban solemnly swore she would stand at the scene of Judgment, whenever that may be. But back then, she had no idea that the heat of the scene would be so searing. On Judgment Day, the world from God's vantage point was too incandescent to behold with dry eyes.

Then, God permitted her tears. Şehriban did not yield, she closed her eyes and took a deep breath. She suddenly remembered Choi Sinhak and looked around. He was blinking absently. He seemed to be speaking to her, but she could not hear anything. She was determined to tune out all sound until the bombs went off—*BOOM! BOOM! BOOM!* Until that moment when Beanstalk would receive God's sentence with all of its body.

It was nearly time. Şehriban wept without meaning to. She waited for what seemed an eternity, standing with her eyes shut. She could hear nothing and could feel nothing—not even gravity, existence, or the floor beneath her feet. How long she stood there, she did not know, but she abruptly came to her senses. She was hungry. How much time had passed? She turned to check the clock. It was already long past the scheduled time. She peered around.

Choi Sinhak said, "It must have been time by now, but it's quiet."

"What did you say?" asked Şehriban

"Nothing's happened. It's well past time. We've been up here for over two hours already." This must have been what he had been saying to her earlier. "The bombs are half an hour late. Maybe you set the timer wrong or …?"

"What? I don't think so. I followed the instructions. I didn't make a mistake," Şehriban answered, but her voice was uncertain. Punctuated by another round of blinking, peace had returned once more.

"Then could it be we're already dead …? No, it couldn't be. Anyway, the staff are telling us to leave. The observatory's closing."

"What? Alright," said Şehriban.

Blink, blink. Nothing happened. On Judgment Day.

Weird, thought Şehriban. *This isn't how it should have gone. I definitely did everything as planned.*

Cosmomafia's assassin must have stolen out of Beanstalk before the bombs were due to explode. Şehriban did not chase after Choi Sinhak. Nor did he, her.

The timer had positively worked, thought Şehriban. *But all six bombs had failed to go off. But at least four, no, two at the very least, should've exploded.*

Şehriban sought out the property owners who had guarded the bombs for sixty-five years. Most of them were still staying in Beanstalk. Each time she met one, they gave a start as soon as they spotted her and struggled to explain themselves.

"I didn't come here to retaliate, don't worry," said Şehriban to one property owner.

"It didn't go off, huh?" the owner said. "I'm sorry."

"You knew beforehand?" Şehriban asked.

"Yes. You could say that."

"Then you did it? I mean, you fiddled with it?"

"Well, you could say that, too, I suppose."

"But why?"

"Because …"

Şehriban thought she might already know the answer.

"… I've watched Beanstalk for six decades while living here," the property owner continued, "and it wasn't Babel. We didn't plot this together or anything. Of course, I did think that one or two people may do what I did. But not *everyone*. I'm sorry none of the bombs exploded—I really didn't see that coming. I thought the others might go through with it, but how could I destroy this place with my own hands? This neighborhood, I mean. I don't know about the whole of Beanstalk, but there was no way I could hurt my neighborhood. I thought it'd be nice if at least the bomb in my home didn't blow up, even if that didn't change anything. Because this place isn't a Tower of Babel."

Fifteen to zero: the decision had been unanimous. Şehriban had nothing else to say. Bombs, detonators, none of them had gone off. The bombs were never going to explode. On Judgment Day, God had handed down a sentence through His jury: probation.

As God blinked absently down at Beanstalk, peace reigned. A true peace that would last for some time.

A year later, Şehriban bought back all fifteen properties from the bank at a slightly higher price than the principal as her contract stated. Technically, it was Cosmomafia that had repaid the bank according to their backdoor deal, but Şehriban had no intention of returning the money to an organization that had abandoned her. She sold all of the properties and became incredibly rich. Her house was soon swimming in bags.

Choi Sinhak's wealth did not change very much, but his mother's did. He spent his life after early retirement helping his mother squander her wealth. He helped her with that a lot. He appeared to finally enjoy the same standard of living as his old pet dog.

And Şehriban and Choi Sinhak never saw each other again.

APPENDIX

Excerpt from
"The Bear God's Afternoon"
by Writer K

Once it rose, the sun was in no hurry to set. One day lasted one year in the Bear God's realm, which remained buried in snow all year long. The Bear God was the evil ruler of night. As the long, long night wore on for half a year, the Bear God would show Themself fleetingly amidst the infinite emptiness and darkness pouring in from the far side of the universe. The Bear God brought a cold blizzard with Them wherever They went. When bitter winds, rasping like the futile breath of the Grim Reaper, tore the ears and reached the heart, all good bears had to retreat into their caves for a seemingly eternal slumber.

But some of the energetic and sensitive bears could not

stand the tedium of night and woke up constantly, tossing and turning. White Bear was one such bear. She was ten years old, already spending her tenth night in the Bear God's realm. She was old enough to be less frightened now by the Bear God's blizzards and the endless abyss of the universe heralding Their arrival. Still, sleep did not come easily to White Bear on that tenth night.

She didn't wonder why. She was just a bear. Instead, White Bear got up and walked toward the cave's entrance. Would there be any food left outside? She dug out the snow and held her head against the hole she had made. An icy wind blasted her face. *Thump-thump*. Her heart, which had slowed down through the night, began to beat faster. She had a feeling it shouldn't. Yet she continued to dig. Was there anything to eat? She was bored. She knew she shouldn't be bored, but she was itching to escape the monotony.

When the hole became big enough to fit her whole head through, White Bear thrust her head outside. The cold snow touched her face. Her body tingled with excitement. She looked up at the sky. It contained nothing. Nothing but the pitch dark. A hollow universe. A hollow darkness, unfathomable as the eyes of prey bleeding hotly to death, crimson against the white ice.

White Bear remembered those eyes. Eyes gazing at somewhere she did not know. Startled, she sometimes looked around in the direction of their gaze. But she would see nothing. On her ninth morning, she sensed intuitively that the place reflected in their eyes was invisible to her, somewhere far, far beyond the world. She realized through those eyes that the place existed. It was likely the Bear God's homeland.

It was such a sky. White Bear was suddenly sad. Her heart beat a little faster. Did sadness make the heart pound? She peered wide-eyed into the abyss shrouding her eyes. The abyss peered into her too. She couldn't tear her eyes away. The abyss was rearing its head.

Without warning, the abyss drew back from her eyes. The blizzard pelted White Bear's face, as if something blocking the cave entrance had vanished.

What was that!

An enormous face materialized out of the abyss. The enormous face had an enormous mouth, nose, and ears. White Bear's heart raced, blood coursing through her body.

A face. It was the face of a pale, colossal bear. The Bear God. White Bear yanked her head out of the hole in alarm. Then, the Bear God pressed Their face against the hole once more. The abyss flooded her vision. Eyes gazing at somewhere beyond the world that was invisible to her. White Bear looked into those eyes. She found it impossible to avoid them. Through them, she saw what she could not see for herself. And at that place where Their blank gaze rested, somewhere far, far beyond the world, she spotted something most unexpected.

What is that? And how did it get over there?

The Bear God was clearly watching her. Her being. The true being inside White Bear that no ordinary bear could see. Fear seized her. A thrill radiated from inside her.

White Bear darted into the cave's depths and crouched. She had to flee. But the night was long and the Bear God stood watch outside the cave. There was no path of escape. Hibernation—one so deep that she might never wake up from it—was the only salvation available to her stricken body. Slowly, very slowly, White Bear fell back asleep.

It was snowing outside the cave when she rose in the morning. It took her a while to wake up. Stretching, she ambled outside the cave and plopped down on the snowy field.

The winds were calm that morning. Light snow descended almost vertically. Nothing else happened in those moments. A mundane time settled on the great earth.

White Bear studied a snowflake that had landed on her forepaw. It had six arms. Another snowflake landed on her forepaw. Another six arms, six identical ones. Yet none of the snowflakes had identical arms to one another. White Bear stood still and waited for a long time. Dozens, hundreds of snowflakes fell endlessly on her paws. How much longer must she wait for the same snowflake to fall? She blinked and pondered. Why did every one of them have different shapes? Who made them? Why make them? Did they mean anything? Did each one have a different meaning?

She considered the snowflakes piled on her paws. There was not one snowflake whose meaning she knew. Looking up, she scanned the snow field before her. Could all that snow have different shapes? She gazed up at the sky, which was filled with flurries. Surely, at least one pair had to be identical when there were so many of them? She lifted her forelegs and stood on two feet. She could see the Bear God's realm reaching far into the distance. The landscape was flat save for one small hill. It was a simple world of universal white. And all of it was supposed to have meaning? The Bear God's realm was full of meanings whose meanings were unknown to her. What could the Bear God's eyes see? Could the Bear God discern the meaning of each and every snowflake?

In the Bear God's realm, where one year was one day, nothing peculiar happened very often. Noticeable changes were hard to see even in broad daylight, or "summer" as people called it. The sun seemed particularly reluctant to set on that long afternoon. Though the snow had stopped falling, meaningless meanings still abounded in the land. White Bear didn't feel like stepping on the snow and walking. But she could not keep lying there. Since her hunting grounds would shrink as the day wore on, that is, as the year wore on, she had to get up and go hunting at every opportunity. This was one of them.

White Bear smelled something. The trace of an entity whose meaning she knew: a dolphin. The winds had carried from afar the hint of a dolphin coming up for air, poking its head out a hole formed in the melting ice. Getting to her feet, White Bear galloped toward the source of the smell, her mighty haunches heaving as she went.

She was in no rush. The dolphin would not swim away just yet. Wide as the sea was under the ice, not all of it was the dolphin's territory. To the dolphin, any part of the sea not touching a sky it could inhale was the domain of death, no matter how plentiful food was there. Dolphins made sure the ice contained breathing holes before venturing into the fertile ocean hidden underneath. And there they were ensnared. A dolphin's breathing hole turned into a trap as soon as White Bear arrived and circled it, unless another breathing hole existed nearby.

Therein lay her conundrum: there were too many breathing holes. The first five days were fine, but the weather had grown too warm from the sixth day. The number of breathing holes surged. White Bear was powerless in such conditions. How would she know which hole her prey would pop up from?

White Bear had run quite a distance when she spotted a breathing hole up ahead. There were no other holes and the ice seemed fairly thick. She was in luck. She couldn't have hoped for more, in fact. She approached the hole and squatted down. When the dolphin appeared, she closed in on it and swiped her forepaw once to intimidate it. Then, she returned to her spot and quietly waited for the dolphin to reappear.

The dolphin was gone a long time. Had it found another hole? It was only after White Bear waited for another long while that the dolphin eventually swam up to the surface, short of breath. Next moment, it vanished back into the water.

Caught you!

White Bear was sure the dolphin had not breathed in enough air. It had probably searched for another hole close by and failed, in which case she did not need to pounce on it so rashly. The longer she drew out the fight, the likelier she was to win it. For the next little while, the dolphin would be unable to poke its head out for a sufficient stretch of time. It would take hurried breaths. A dolphin that didn't breathe in enough of the sky was bound to tire at some point. It would take more risks in desperation. Until then, she had nothing to do but to prowl around the area.

White Bear lapsed back into thought. The dolphin's scent filled the air. She knew it well. The smell of dolphin. The smell of red. It had an explicit meaning too: food. But another thought occurred to her. Just as those white things were not all the same, perhaps every red smell was distinct.

The dolphin stuck its head out of the water then quickly swam away. White Bear had watched the same scene a hundred times before. Of course, she had not seen such a perfect trap these last few days, but she had done this hunt scores of times during her ten days in the Bear God's realm. And yet, was this hunt the same as the other hunts? Were the scores of dolphins she had eaten all the same dolphins? Somehow, she didn't think they were. They couldn't be. She knew perfectly well that she was a different bear from the other bears. If bears were like that, so must be dolphins. Then what meaning did this particular dolphin have? What meaning did *she* have? The answer to the last question was simple. Her ultimate meaning was herself. She didn't need special markings on her to know that much. Then what in the world did that dolphin mean?

The dolphin was fighting frantically for its life. But not White Bear. She waited and waited. She had time, unlike the dolphin.

The dolphin circled the hole in the ice, looking like it was running out of breath. Its movements were plainly tired, as it had surreptitiously swum up and down for so long under White Bear's watchful eye. It wasn't even swimming in deep waters now. One good smack with her paw would be sufficient. Of course, she would have to jump into the water at one point but it would be absurd to lose her long-awaited prey for fear of getting wet. However, she was reluctant.

White Bear quietly stared into the hole. The dolphin was swimming into deeper waters. A moment later, the ground a little way off resounded with a thud. The dolphin seemed to have decided to smash the ice. White Bear jumped to her feet. She could no longer sit idly. Hunting the dolphin would be impossible once the ice broke. The next time it appeared, she would have to dive into the water no matter what.

She didn't want to do that. But she had to. In the end she didn't—she had seen the dolphin's eyes.

White Bear gave up on her hunt. Hungry as she was, there was nothing to be done. She curled up, quietly withdrawing into her thoughts.

Three days and three nights. Though the Bear God's realm didn't switch between day and night very often, that was how much time had passed—time measured by how long it took the sun to complete one sweeping lap around the sky. White Bear had meditated for all three days. Days in which the sun refused to set for half a year once risen, nights in which it refused to rise for half a year once set. The world was still cold, but the afternoon was not frigid enough to thicken the now-thin sheet of ice. The afternoon was when the Bear God's power slowly waned.

The first thing White Bear did each morning was go out of her cave and survey the Bear God's realm. She could see at a glance that Their realm had grown noticeably smaller. Some of the sea ice had been pushed onto land. Ice not covering the sea was useless for it could not serve as a hunting ground.

White Bear munched on seaweed washed up on the thawed land. Sometimes the dizzying smell of prey filled her nose, but there was no point chasing it now. All she would find was the sea, not a hole in the ice. Even if she did find a hole, it would be no use. If the ice wasn't thick enough to support White Bear's mighty haunches, it was as good as a valley of death to her.

The other bears, like White Bear, lost more and more weight. White Bear resumed the meditation she had done for three days. As her once-massive body grew lighter, the cold became harder to stand, yet her mind at least felt more at ease with each passing day.

White Bear followed the dolphins. Although a myriad of dolphins swam around in the ocean, White Bear remembered the one she had met three days ago. Carefully, she observed the dolphins, all of them similar yet varying slightly. They smelled different from that dolphin and looked different too. Why were they different? What did that mean?

Sometimes White Bear encountered a dolphin caught in a trap, underneath a hole in an ice crust that had grown as thin as ever. All energy had been sapped from White Bear already. While she could jump into the water and attempt to hunt, she had just one chance left. If she failed, she didn't think she would have the strength to climb back onto the ice. She had thought she was bound to win this fight with the passing of time, but no. She was bound to lose if time passed without her hunting anything.

Despite her last chance slipping away before her eyes, White Bear had no desire to hunt. Well, she did have some desire. Only, what she wished to hunt had changed. Instead of searching for food, she wanted to search for something else. She was still hungry but reluctant to eat the flesh of a dead dolphin to satiate her hunger. She wanted to eat something else, but what? And what must she do to eat it?

It was all she could do to stand on the thin ice. She peered down. A dolphin pushed its head out an ice hole. It could flee or it could move to another hole. But it did neither. It probably knew how frail White Bear was. Looking at the dolphin, White Bear sensed that her death was near. She had seen her pitiful reflection in the dolphin's eyes.

White Bear was gripped not by the fear of death but by the questions that had plagued her for three days. *Who are you? I don't need markings on me to know I am special, a bear different from the others, but who are you? How do I find out if you are special too? Who am I even talking to right now?*

At that moment, the ice she was standing on split into two with a loud crack. She tumbled straight into the water. She kicked her weak legs to scramble up onto the ice, but the ice her paws pushed down on kept splintering. It felt impossible to hoist herself up.

I should give up.

Relaxing her body, White Bear let herself float. Her temperature dropped. Her heart seemed to slow down. She was only falling asleep though. What did she have to fear? But how long would she have to sleep? Bears didn't know that the duration of night was the same as that of day. They had to stay awake all night to find out how long it was, but no bear could do so. Whenever White Bear drifted off to her winter sleep, she thought she might never wake up again. She also dreaded that the Bear God's realm might melt while she slept, allowing Them to find her.

Her strength had left her. As she floated limply on the water, her eyes naturally settled on the sky. It was snowing. A snowflake landed on the tip of her nose. It was cold. She wasn't supposed to feel anything, yet her legs shivered from the sensation.

That was when White Bear became snow. Snow that vanished as soon as it touched the water. Her body seemed to melt away, little by little. Was she imagining it? All of her turned into snow before long and engulfed the Bear God's realm. Her snowflakes only had four arms. Four arms and one head. None of the myriad snowflakes looked alike. When she piled herself layer upon layer to form a sheet of ice, dolphins knocked against her from below. *Thud. Thud. Thump-thump.*

She came around. She was still in the water. *Thump-thump*, her heart must not have fallen asleep yet. She watched the swirling snowstorm as her existence slowly faded. Dolphins swam around her. The thunderous blows of the great Whale God slamming into the Bear God's land traveled through the sea and shook her heart. She could not tell the sound apart from her own heartbeat.

Thump-thump. Something made the sound. White Bear didn't think it was her heartbeat at first, but she realized it had a regular rhythm. She listened intently, her eyelids sliding shut. It was dark. Pitch-black night. She heard the sound of infinite darkness pouring down.

Pik-pik-pik. It sounded like something tiny was scratching the ground. Tiny as a snowflake. White Bear drew nearer and looked down. A small hole appeared, so small she could hardly see it. She pushed her face toward it. A little closer, a little closer. When she came close enough to cover the hole completely, she pressed one eye against it and spotted a creature digging its way out of the hole. Eyes, nose, mouth, ears. It was a white bear with a long face. The small bear looked up at her in alarm.

You're!

White Bear lifted her head, startled. Then, the small bear, also startled, withdrew its face from the hole. White Bear recognized the small bear even in the pitch dark. *I know who you are.* Four legs and one head. A bear different from any other bear, a snowflake shaped differently from any other snowflake, a one-of-a-kind being that could never pass by her unnoticed, no matter how small, no matter how quiet.

You're!

Me!

She opened her eyes. She was assuming a skyward position again. Snowflakes flew at her face.

Can the Bear God discern the meaning of each and every snowflake?

To the question of her life that she'd had three days ago, to herself who had asked that question to goodness knows who, she nodded and replied:

Yes, They can.

Really? But who on earth are you? Who are you to reply to me?

Me? I am the only bear that can keep my eyes open all night.

She asked, *Really? Who can do that?*

She answered, *Who do you think? The Bear God.*

The Bear God entered nirvana that afternoon. The great Bear God's afternoon, when the sun never sets.

Café Beans Talking

*Excerpt from the Introduction
to* A Study on Level 520

"Measures to Spatialize Planar Constituencies" proposes to restructure constituencies that span horizontally into three-dimensional ones resembling cubes. As an experiment by Beanstalk Tacit Power Research has proven, word of mouth from face-to-face interactions spreads decisively faster across the same floor than it does between floors. The message conveyed also has a much more persuasive effect when spread horizontally, rather than vertically.

This discovery has attracted a lot of attention in association with elections. That verticalists have never won the City Council elections despite their complete domination of newspapers, TV, and other major media outlets is closely related to the size of the Beanstalk Council. With a total of 199 councilors in Beanstalk, one councilor represents only an average of 2,652.47 citizens. Therefore, on average a candidate who receives 1,327 votes is guaranteed victory regardless of voter demographics or voter turnout, and 557 votes in an election with a sixty-percent voter turnout is likely to win regardless of the other candidates' tallies. In fact, those elected to the Twelfth Council had only won a mere 472.2 votes on average.

In Beanstalk, mass media is the most effective means of shifting public opinion. This is true here just as it is in any other country. The problem for verticalists however is the number 473—it is too small to be called the public. Word of mouth is often more successful than mass media in capturing the hearts of 473 people.

As a result, verticalists have persistently attempted to cut the total number of Council seats. If the average number of votes a councilor has to obtain increases, mass media would have a greater influence on elections. A vertical expansion of a constituency would have the same effect. Rather than one word-of-mouth network corresponding to one constituency, multiple word-of-mouth networks existing in relative isolation across one constituency gives mass media an advantage. But the odds of the constituency map ever changing are slim unless verticalists win an overwhelming majority.

Bicey was dispatched to Level 520 by the verticalists to conduct research for devising a new campaign strategy. The neighborhood I lived in at the time belonged to a typical planar constituency that was only three levels high despite being hundreds of meters in length and width. So, the verticalists hypothesized that finding out how word of mouth travelled on Level 520 would offer clues to understanding the rest of Beanstalk's informal networks.

"Isn't it funny," Bicey said to me. "My boss told me to live here for about six months and join Level 520's word-of-mouth network. I asked her, 'What about rent? Will I get research funds?' But she just said her tenant's supposed to move out soon so I should just live there. She didn't even give me the place for free. She told me she'd lower the rent, but it wasn't that cheap when I got here. I couldn't do anything about it though. I either had to do as I was told or leave the organization. That's how I ended up here."

Bicey was a researcher at Beanstalk Tacit Power Research. Her real name was Jin Gyunghee, and she was a thirty-six-year-old single woman. Bicey quickly became a part of Level 520's word-of-mouth network without realizing it—not as a subject but as an object. Barely two weeks after Bicey had moved to Level 520, I heard a rumor about the appearance of a suspicious woman, who turned out to be Bicey. The epicenter of the rumor was the gym at the local community center. As Yunsoo (female, aged thirty-six at the time) put it: "Isn't she a little weird? Not just weird, fishy, more like. Why is she hanging around with that lot? I mean, she looks perfectly sane. What did she used to do? She dresses weird too."

I observed Bicey closely. She didn't seem to understand the ecosystem of the Level 520 gym at all. For example, women on Level 520 rarely wore shorts at the gym in those days. The dress code was sweatpants with a plain t-shirt, and the preferred workout was running or yoga over weight-lifting. Women with short hair usually wore a headband, socks were typically white or yellow, and the pre-workout drink of choice was black coffee. Such practices had no special reason; it was simply the current trend. Bicey did none of what we did. She was evidently from out of town.

Even stranger was her signing up for the gym's regular meetups, which were dominated by middle-aged men. Other gym members in their twenties and thirties never mingled with middle-aged men—they neither chatted to them nor said hello, and even had the tendency to use separate fitness equipment. The female members might have all rushed to a gender-segregated gym, if only there had been one.

Jihyun (female, twenty-two), my neighbor and a college student, testified as such about the middle-aged male gym-goers: "Why do I avoid them? Well, I guess they're scary for one. They come stampeding into the gym in those weird-colored shorts and work out huffing and puffing. Calling each other 'Mr. Lee,' 'Mr. Park,' guffawing their heads off. After they're done huffing and puffing for all the world to see, they go for barbeque together."

Other people had similar views. My gym friends and I were therefore horrified when one day we spotted Bicey tagging along with the huffer-and-puffers on their way to have barbeque.

Bicey later said, "Why did I tag along? I had to. It was for work. Word of mouth starts in places like that. What choice did I have when that's what I came here to do? I wouldn't find anything useful by following young people around.

Think about it. What good would it do to hang out with people who go straight home when they've done their workout?"

Apart from middle-aged men, none of the other demographic groups in the gym formed social gatherings just because they went to the same gym. It was also unimaginable for people who finished working out at the same time to hit the showers together, and no one talked when they ran into each other in the shower room. Bicey was of course an exception.

What earned Bicey her nickname was her overzealous passion for weight training, a workout which other young women rarely did at the gym.

"At this rate, just her biceps are going to be huge," Yunsoo observed. "She should tone her triceps too. I don't get how she does the same thing over and over. I bet you her arms will become so humongous she won't be able to fit them through the arm holes of a t-shirt."

Yunsoo was initially wary of Bicey, but they ended up forming a close friendship. Still, they didn't time their showers together or anything of the sort. Bicey was unhappy about that.

"Can't you help out a friend?" Bicey ended up pleading. "I need to collect *some* information."

"But you're barking up the completely wrong tree," Yunsoo responded. "I've been working out here for five years and I've never seen anyone talk politics. What on earth were you imagining? In other neighborhoods, do people talk to each other in the gym showers or something?"

"How should I know? I've never been."

That was why Yunsoo took Bicey to Café Beans Talking,

a coffee shop located near the freight elevator terminal on Standard Level 521. The small vacant lot in front of the café was considered the de facto "nerve center" of Level 520's word-of-mouth network. That is of course just an expression used by researchers; to borrow the words of locals, the lot was something of a rumor mill.

Café Beans Talking was not your regular coffee shop. It was originally a freight distribution center shared by local horizontal labor unions. The owner of the café, Jang Samnam (male, fifty-seven), was a former member of the area's horizontal labor union who, after suffering major injuries to his left leg, began selling coffee near the union with its permission.

As Jang explained: "I was devastated. Apart from making deliveries, I didn't know how to do anything. I started selling coffee with no shop, no nothing. Back then, the sort of coffee you see today was rare. I basically sold instant coffee. My coffee wasn't one bit better than vending-machine coffee. It probably tasted worse. But business was good. Real good. After a year or two, I was earning more than what my old job used to pay. Why? The union members all bought coffee from me. They did it for no reason. They just bought a cup whenever they passed by."

Jang opened a shop with his increased earnings and stocked it with a coffee machine. But his coffee was still bad. It tasted so bland that true coffee lovers hardly ever came to his shop. Instead, it was cheaper than other coffee shops. Jang knew full well who was keeping his business alive, and he had no ambitions to make a fortune from selling coffee. Beans

Talking became a space for all union members.

Lee Sang-eun (female, forty-two) confirmed: "We drop by when we're bored. I reckon we visit at least twice a day. We sit and unwind here after work and pop by on weekends. No one tells us off for sitting here without ordering a coffee. We hang out here a lot because it'd be better than getting wasted. This is where we meet people." As Lee said, Beans Talking was a social space and a recreation center for union members, and with time, grew into a sanctuary for all residents of Level 520.

Hwang Jong-jae (male, thirty-nine), another union member, offered a similar viewpoint: "Rumors? Yeah, this is the best place to hear 'em. We come and go to every nook and cranny on Level 520 umpteen times a day for work, you know. Park yourself here the whole day, and you'll get the lowdown on everything that's happening on Level 520."

Bicey's face brightened when she heard about Beans Talking, as if she had found her answer. She began to show up at the gym less frequently. The gym gang, including myself, didn't realize what that meant for months.

Then one day, a year before the City Council elections, the largest takeout coffee chain in Beanstalk, Queen's Terrace, opened three branches on Levels 519 to 521, one on each floor. Its coffee was fifty percent more expensive than Café Beans Talking's, but it was offering a launch promotion during which you could buy coffee for a slightly cheaper price than at Beans Talking. It was running the promotion for six months—it meant to price Beans Talking out of the market.

The residents of Level 520, of course, raved about Queen's

Terrace. We completely failed to understand why the chain had decided to wage a self-destructive price war for six months, nor did we even try to understand. In addition to selling much stronger, richer coffee than Beans Talking, Queen's Terrace offered an incomparable variety of coffee beans. The younger generation was the first to leave Beans Talking, the rest followed soon after. Queen's Terrace promptly opened another branch on Level 521. Opening multiple branches was not a problem for Queen's Terrace—as it specialized in take-out orders, the real estate costs of all four branches combined were worth less than Café Beans Talking. Queen's Terrace had slightly cheaper, better coffee, but no space to enjoy the coffee at your leisure.

We would buy coffee together at Queen's Terrace before scattering to our individual spaces. We couldn't bring that coffee to Beans Talking and chat there. Of course, those whose palates were insensitive to different coffees continued to gather at the gym, huff and puff in a furious workout, swarm the shower room at the same time, go for barbeque as a group at least twice a week, and visit Café Beans Talking as they always had, oblivious to what had changed. But other types of people could not do that.

Instead, we went our separate ways to the properties we each occupied, in which we were tamed anew by the sweet thrills of mass media. Café Beans Talking closed down, and the word-of-mouth network of Level 520 disappeared all too easily. In just one year, we had gone from being people of Level 520 to people of Beanstalk.

And so came the City Council election. A horizontalist

candidate lost to a verticalist candidate for the first time ever in the Level 520 constituency: 389 votes to 422. I didn't realize what that entailed at the time. The verticalists won an unprecedented landslide victory in that year's elections. I didn't realize what that entailed either.

It took a year for the realization to hit me. With the closure of Café Beans Talking, the lives on Level 520 somehow lost some of their humanity. We began to avert our eyes even when we saw someone we clearly knew, as if all our neighbors had suddenly turned into city folk. We were no longer interested in each other's personal lives. "Rumors everyone knew about" ceased to exist. Yunsoo didn't even remember who Bicey was. This was one year after Bicey vanished.

All because Café Beans Talking was gone. The election strategy Bicey discovered had hit the nail on the head. Face-to-face networks losing their influence and mass media replacing them—that was what had transformed Level 520 into a less friendly place.

The problem was not limited to Level 520. Similar things happened in various parts of Beanstalk around the same time. Local communities on most floors tended to have naturally-formed hubs of activity. And the hubs tended to eventually die out. People accepted that fact without question, believing hubs naturally appeared and then disappeared. But this is not true. Beanstalk's horizontal local communities disappeared almost at the same time. So, many local communities simultaneously lost their hubs around when Café Beans Talking went out of business.

But the people who belonged to these horizontal local

communities didn't notice because there were no networks binding them together. That realization was what led to the creation of the Horizontalist Alliance and in some cases morphed into contradictory approaches like Separatist Unity. All such events had arisen because we had failed to defend Café Beans Talking.

My motivation for writing this book shares a similar concern. If we cannot defend Level 520, what is there may also disappear for good. The number 520 will not be erased of course, but Level 520 as the setting of our daily lives, not as a vertical coordinate marking a point in the three-dimensional space of Beanstalk, may be wiped clean from everyone's memories forever unless someone documents it like I attempt to do in this book. This book is thus not a record of the facts or ideologies my colleagues and I have studied, but a record of our treasured lives and everyday experiences that extended horizontally across the spaces of Level 520.

In the hope that those lives will be remembered for years to come, I discuss in Chapter 1 …

A "Crazy" Interview with Actor P, Who Understands Interiority

So you've just won an award.

Yes. It was a special one, the first acting award given to a nonhuman actor.

You seem to be attaching a lot of meaning to the fact that the award went to a "nonhuman actor."

Of course. I think competing with human actors as equals is commendable, but that's not the end goal. Because you're ultimately a prop for their movies. The award I received means more than that. It implies that as an actor I have pioneered new acting territory never explored by human actors.

You didn't win in the competitive categories. Does that upset you?

No. The fact that I won the Honorary Award instead of Best Actor means they've recognized that the criteria of human film festivals can't judge my performance and that I should be judged at a film festival for animals, if there were one. But as you know, there is no such thing. I believe they've shown me the highest form of respect in the present circumstances. Their message was that they couldn't help but laud my performance even if it was beyond their scope of evaluation, and I sympathize with that message.

Your acceptance speech was impressive.

You think so? It was an Honorary Award so I couldn't prepare anything. It caught me completely off guard because I'd never even won in competitive categories like Rising Star or Best Actor before. There was something I had meant to say though, not for this festival per se, but in case I did get up on stage for a similar honor someday. But my mind drew a blank when I actually got up there.

What did you mean to say?

Woof woof woof.

What did you actually say?

Woof woof.

Was that enough? You must've had plenty of help along the way, so you could have given some shout-outs. A typical acceptance speech isn't always the way to go, but I suspect your speech left some disappointed.

Of course. I had so many friends I wanted to thank. But it couldn't be helped. As you know, I don't speak human. As a matter of fact, I think this interview is also crazy. When my manager told me about this interview, I honestly thought she was joking so I said sure. Then, this happened. I had no idea I was really going to do an interview.

Your manager is answering on your behalf. Are you happy with her answers? Are there any discrepancies with your own views?

I am happy with her answers. I trust her. She knows me so well. She's worked with me ever since I debuted. Things would've been very difficult without her. I would've continued working in this field, but it sure would've been very difficult. Communicating with the director or other crew members is a critical issue for an actor, especially an actor like myself. Apart from needing to discuss my understanding of the work, oftentimes I'd have problems with the most trivial matters. Since humans don't have a strong sense of smell, they would sometimes demand highly emotional acting from me in environments where I found it almost impossible to work. I would be in great discomfort if such problems weren't taken care of.

I heard working conditions were even worse when you started out.

Back then I had no script, no storyboard. I went into shoots without knowing which scene we were filming when the rest of the cast knew. The Direction Department used things like rubber balls or dog gum to coach my acting. For example, while everyone was running around looking for decisive evidence of a crime, I would have to concentrate on finding a toy rubber ball. But I could not for the life of me concentrate in that environment. In the third *Scent Sleuth* movie, there is a scene where drug squad detective Oh Jayoung is attacked by a drug gang and dies, but if you look closely you can see me wagging my tail. It's a terribly mortifying scene for me, but it wasn't really my fault.

Nonetheless you managed to cement your reputation as an actor through that film. Your performance was so good I could hardly believe that was your first role.

I wouldn't say so. All I actually did at the time were action scenes. Human directors didn't ask for subtle emotional acting from animal actors. They assumed we could adequately convey feelings by wagging our tail, perking up our ears, or blinking. So, in the early days, nonhuman actors with only four or five expressions were lauded for putting on a stellar emotional performance. Acting wasn't so difficult in those conditions. I just had to pull off the action, which I happened to have a knack for.

No need to be so modest. You were showered with praise for your incredible action sequences, and everyone still remembers your performance. What was your secret for success?

I didn't have any. But I was at an advantage when I started out. The actor who was originally cast in the lead role for *Scent Sleuth* was not from Beanstalk. As a performer, they were incomparably better than I was, but they had some trouble doing stunts. Having received acting training in the neighboring country, I think they had a hard time adapting to filming in three-dimensional spaces. It's an understandable problem, really. I also struggle to adapt when acting in vast two-dimensional spaces.

Chase scenes being trendy at the time, most of the movie comprised of running all over Beanstalk. I had no problem navigating different levels as I was born and bred in Beanstalk. I caught the director's eye just when the original actor for the part was having a rough time. I got lucky. I did a running audition on set and was cast right off the bat. That was the moment my life changed completely.

Have you ever had regrets?

For the most part, no. But I do have a few regrets.

What are they?

I forgot what it feels like to not be recognized by anyone. I often want to walk around the square by myself on a normal weekday afternoon or on a weekend. But I never get the chance. I don't think I ever will. The thought makes me sad.

Do you have the same issue with dating?

Yes, definitely. But dating is a little different. Ironically, we animal actors are a lot more vulnerable to scandal than human actors. A scandal can hurt our image to the extent of finishing our careers. This has to do with the fact that Beanstalk, though its inhabitants loathe the comparison, is often compared to Babel or sometimes even to ancient cities like

Sodom and Gomorrah. Because Sodom is associated with bestiality, when animal actors fall in love with humans, our romantic relationships are too often seen as sordid bestiality. It's so unfair, but that is our reality. And an actor who has such associations eventually gets forced out of the industry. So, we can't remain naïve. This isn't a matter of strategy, but a matter of survival.

Still, love has no boundaries. Some loves you can't give up on even when you know they will be misunderstood. Have you ever found such love?
I don't want to answer that.

There seems to be a lot more emotional depth to your performances lately. That look you just had in your eyes, I've seen it onscreen too. Is real life inspiring your acting these days?
Naturally. Once your acting career takes off, your life begins to veer from the ordinary trajectory of life, which I think is a tremendous loss to you as an actor. Becoming a star, earning a fortune, and living in a great house aren't necessarily bad. But not every actor should live like that. If all actors lose touch with reality and only experience the wretchedness of life on the streets in movies, then cinema and television would be doomed. But I'm caught in that same trap. I act out sadness, experiencing it only during the few months of shooting. The rest of the time I have fun. Sometimes I over-immerse myself in sadness to make up for those shortcomings. But the sadness I squeeze out of myself is far from real sadness. That's my regret. And that regret has piled up slowly but surely like

the weight of time to become a sort of mirror reflecting my interiority. I believe my current self is far more beautiful than my healthy self when I was a rookie.

I agree. What made you famous may have been your elaborate action sequences in Scent Sleuth, *but I think hands down what made you a top actor was your quiet, emotional performance in* Low Nose.

Low Nose is a blessing of a work for me. While I was filming it, I didn't feel like myself. There were moments when I was shocked by my own portrayal. I don't think I could ever pull off that kind of performance again even if someone asked me to. You don't always do a better job when you're given more time. The film taught me that and was clear proof I still had room for change.

What was the most memorable scene for you?

Definitely the last one. It was also my last shoot. The moment I performed my last line, I felt as though something inside me slipped out of my body. I can't forget that moment.

What was the line? Can I ask you to reenact it?

"Woof." It was a succinct line. As I just said, it's impossible to reenact. Now and forever.

You've risen to the top. Any areas you'd like to challenge yourself in going forward?

I have no plans to try new things. I'm content with the work I'm doing now. I've experienced something not everybody can experience and have had more than enough fun doing my job. You have no idea how relieved I am that this isn't goodbye. I'm infinitely blessed to have more days of acting in store for me.

Any last words for our readers?
  Woof-woof! Woof-woof!

Author's Note

I thought I had written everything there was to write when I realized there was still the Author's Note. The narrators of my stories hastily clocked out the instant I finished the manuscript, and whatever I write now must sound like a letter of apology, but perhaps that is precisely why this is the moment to write an Author's Note.

Someone once told me that good-humored people never become writers. That people who nurse grudges and write them down when nobody is looking instead of immediately talking them out are the ones that become writers.

There are three things people told me that I nursed in my heart while writing this book. The first was a harsh piece of criticism, the gist of which was "I don't really want to read a joke like this and it's not even funny." They thought I was *joking*? I was cross the whole day I heard that, but I just stored the words irritably in my heart.

The second was, "I was about to leave on a journey, but I've decided to wait a little more because of this book." To me, this sounded like "I was about to leave this world, but I've decided to put off my decision for a bit." I don't know how serious the person was when they said it, but being a writer, I had to store those words too.

The last was something my editors said. At some point, they began to refer to this book as "our book" and the words stayed with me. They worked hard enough to call it that and were sometimes brimming with more inspiration than I was.

Those were the words that kept me nervous while I wrote this book. I'm not sure if writing about my nervousness will lessen the entirety of its weight, but I should stop holding grudges until I find new words to store in my heart.

Thank you to the many people who helped, and I wish good health to His Excellency Mr. L, who is my infinite source of inspiration. I owe special, inexpressible gratitude to my long-time friend and advocate, Juhi.

Bae Myung-hoon

honfordstar.com